Growing Up Barksdale:
A True Baltimore Story

To my mother, Joan Carlene,
who told me it is okay to be different

Authors' Note

The book you are holding is the result of a collaboration between two Baltimoreans, one a student of writing and one with a famous last name and a gift for storytelling. After crossing paths in a ride-sharing service in September 2016, Grace and Dante decided to undertake the project of writing Dante's remarkable life story.

Over the span of many months, Dante told Grace his story via audio-recorded interviews, which she then transcribed and edited in a Google document. With shared access to the document, Dante made corrections to Grace's language, filled in gaps in the story, and patiently answered the questions of someone who, despite growing up less than four miles away, knew next to nothing about the world he inhabits.

Into this story so many others are woven—it is as much the story of one man as it is a slice of Baltimore's history and a reckoning with its present.

Prologue
March, 1974

My mother says God sent the stray dogs. It was early spring and she was nine months pregnant, waiting outside her building for an ambulance that wasn't on its way. Calling 911 from Lafayette projects was like writing a letter to Santa Claus.

Sirens whirred in the distance and she thought of her two sons. They were only four and five, too young for the sound to make her wonder where they were. That morning, when her water broke, she had roused her first-born out of a deep sleep.

"Woody, wake up your brother and go up Aunt Kitty's. I need to go to the hospital."

Kitty was her brother Richard's girlfriend. They lived on the seventh floor.

"I'm 'sleep, Mom! I don't wanna go…"

An empty Bugles bag skidded across Aisquith Street. For a moment, she wished she had let the boys stay with her. It was one thing to be alone on the street in the early hours of the morning, and another to be alone on the street, and in labor.

Fear had just begun to crystallize in her mind when the first dog appeared. It approached slowly and rubbed against her legs. She usually shooed strays away, but as this one lay at her feet she felt protected. As if God was watching that morning when she stepped outside. As if He saw her now, leaning back against the brick, feeling warm and then cold, body stretched tight to hold another one inside.

Before long, there were a dozen strays gathered. And when the ambulance didn't come, and she had to call a cab, the dogs formed a circle around her. They wouldn't let the driver near. Like shepherds through the valley of the shadow of death, they escorted my mother to the car.

Part I

1

The Projects

"Your mother so dumb," I shouted, "I told her it was chilly outside and she went and got a spoon!"

There was laughter from the street.

"Yo, look at goofy ass Odell!" called Shang. He was four years older than me and better at hitting where it hurt. We were leaning on the fence of the balcony, taunting the low-rise boys below. One of them yelled something in response, but we couldn't hear him from eleven stories up.

It was a Saturday in late October and Lafayette projects towered over East Baltimore. You can say what you want about Lafayette but we had the raw views of the city. From where I stood with Shang, we could see across the whole Inner Harbor, all the way to the Francis Scott Key Bridge.

My family lived on the fourth floor of 131 Aisquith Street. All the high-rises were the same height, but 131 building was the best because it faced all the others. When I came up here, the whole complex lay below me.

Down in the courtyard, the other 131 boys were beefing with the 200 building boys. I could just make out Crutty Mone's skinny arm around somebody else's neck, and Dietrich's body bent double in laughter. Crutty Mone and his twin Michael lived below me, on the third floor. Like a lot of families, theirs would move to the low-rises once more siblings came along. Dee lived on the seventh floor with his mother, Ms. Nita. Ms. Nita was a single parent. I never saw her mess with anyone but Dee's little sister's father.

I could see Leon standing a few feet back from the tussle. He and Dee were both couple years younger than the rest of us, but only Leon was still a crybaby. He and his mother lived in the low-rises. Leon had one of them real pretty mothers, Ms. Diane was her name, which fit 'cause she looked like Diana Ross. Ms. Diane messed with the big hustlers, so Leon always had name-brand everything.

It looked like Mone was about to get that ass beat when Dee finally straightened himself and swung a fist. I let out a whoop from my perch.

Here's what you have to understand about Lafayette projects—it was always rivalries between the buildings. We settled things by fighting. I probably fought every one of my friends. Walking past the 7/11 or the McDonald's parking lot, you might get a water balloon thrown at your face, or a "Wassup" in the wrong tone of voice, and then it'd be on. Dudes who didn't want to beef stayed in the house.

The boy that Dee hit turned around at the sound of my yell, and I saw it was my homeboy Jerome. That was the other thing about Lafayette projects—we were all friends.

On the other side of Aisquith Street, the older boys were playing basketball in front of 1101 building. One of them was about ten inches shorter than everyone else on the court, and we watched as he ducked underneath an outstretched arm and went smooth into a lay-up. While not yet a household name in the rest of America, Muggsy Bogues was already famous in East Baltimore.

Waiting below the basket for his rebound was Reggie Williams, also fifteen, but taller than any grown man I knew. Reggie lived next door to us in 131. We called him Russ. He and Mugs were sophomores at Dunbar High School, in the same class as Reggie Lewis and one grade below David Wingate. With that starting line-up, the Dunbar Poets were about to win the next fifty-nine games they played and be ranked first in the country by the end of the season. People like to give Bob Wade, the Dunbar coach, all the credit for that

125 building

Playing basketball outside the low-rises

team, but really the NBA owes a debt to Mr. Leon Howard, the projects' basketball coach and a surrogate father for a lot of those guys.

Lucky for the chubby kids like me, Lafayette also had a football league. Each building had its own team, and we played on the fields throughout the projects and across from the McDonald's and 7/11. But that was only practice for the real football team, the Lafayette Raiders, ages 10-12 and 12-14. Mr. Howard coached us, too, and every season ended with a championship. If you made it into the picture that hung in 7/11, you became a project hero.

"Look at Odell big goofy ass!" Shang shouted again, but Odell and the other low-rise boys had lost interest. I was getting hungry anyway, and I told Shang so. He launched a glob of spit through the bars of the fence, and then turned and ducked through the door to the stairwell. 131 might have had the best location, but our stairs smelled like piss like all the others. Sometimes we rode the counterweight in the elevator from the fifth floor to the top, but I hadn't gone in since my boy Williams got crushed between the elevator car and the wall and broke both his legs and an arm.

Back in the apartment, my mom was arguing with Uncle Rebo, who lived down Perkins projects. Uncle Rebo was my father's younger brother.

"No, how many times I have to tell you? I don't need you looking after them." As she talked, she fumbled with her key ring, trying to remove the house key. "Here, can you get this— I'm late for my shift."

"It was two years ago, Carlene!" He took the key ring and turned it in his hands. "Just let me take 'em over 7/11. Y'all want hotdogs, boys?"

My mother rolled her eyes. She was clearly thinking about the last time she left me under Uncle Rebo's care. That day, the playground behind 125 building had felt like a mile from home. I had crawled underneath the slide and was watching him pretend to look for me. He was checking the inside of a tunnel when we both heard a voice call out, "Testers!"

As soon as that word rang out, people started running from all directions toward the sound. They were pushing and shoving and tripping over each other's feet, it looked like a riot breaking out. My uncle called out for me to stay put for a minute, and then he took off running.

Before I even realized I was alone, I felt my mother's grip on my arm. She was screaming after Uncle Rebo. *You just gon' leave him out here?! Don't come get my fucking son anymore!*

Now she looked over at me, hand wrist-deep in a box of cereal. Shang was browsing the contents of the refrigerator.

"I got to work. Pop's coming to get you." She laid the house key on the kitchen table.

"Lock the door behind you," she continued. "And don't be dirtying up my damn house. We have a tenant council meeting tonight and Granny and Ike and me got work to do for this dinner we giving at the rec."

My mother was on the tenant council for Lafayette projects. Mr. Ike was the council president, and Granny was his wife. The council was supposed to be a kind of liaison between the residents and the housing administration office—like if someone's toilet broke and the maintenance man never came—but they were also the unofficial fundraisers. It was always a bake sale happening, or a raffle, or a potluck dinner at the rec. Most of the time, the money went toward things like Free Lunch. But if they raised enough, we got to go on field trips. A few weeks earlier, we'd all been to an Orioles game at Memorial Stadium.

Moms also worked at the McDonald's on the corner of Fayette and Central. Back then, Mr. Sherman had the 7/11, Mr. Gerry had the Amaco gas station, and Ms. Merriweather had the McDonald's. She hired all the ladies from the projects when she opened. She ended up regretting that decision though, 'cause my mother and the other project moms used to feed us. Didn't matter who you were, my mother might just pass you like twenty hamburgers over the counter on your way home from school. And as it turned out, Ms. Merriweather wasn't running no Free Lunch program.

After my mother left, shooing Uncle Rebo out with her, Shang pulled a shoebox out from under the bed. Inside was a brand new pair of shell-head Adidas, bright enough to blind you. Shang was on that Adidas tip even before Run-D.M.C., when tennis shoes were still named after actual tennis players. He knew better than to wear them in front of our mother, though.

"Where you goin'?" I asked, as Shang unlaced his sneakers.

"I gotta go watch the building," he said. Shang was the lookout for two dealers named Kevin and Ock over at 1101 building. His job was to stand outside the building and call out *Linda, Linda!* or whatever if he saw police coming. Kevin and Ock paid him 250 dollars a day to do that, which is how he could afford whatever brand of sweatsuit or tennis shoe mattered. He had the Jordache jeans, the Sergio Valentes, the Herman Survivors, the sheepskin coats, the leather Westwind jackets. He was just about the slickest ten-year-old you ever saw.

Shang stood up and pulled his hood over his head. "Holla at you later," he called, and was out the door.

I ate my cereal and watched from the window as Shang dashed across Aisquith Street to 1101 building, his backpack slung over one shoulder, his feet white as teeth. It was unusual for oldheads like Kevin and Ock to employ someone so young, but Shang was an unusual kid. He was one of those people who could emerge unscathed from almost any situation, holding whatever it was he wanted in a balled-up fist. He was an enforcer of his own will. He just got through that way. In our teenage years, when Woody would get in trouble for staying out too late, he'd beef with my mother about it. *Whatchu gonna say to Shang?* he'd ask. *He out right now!* She would make excuses for him, say he had mental health problems—he was beyond her control, in other words.

On the steps of 1101 building, Shang nodded to Uncle Butt

Butt. Butt Butt was one of Moms' brothers. He was pretty much king of the projects, everybody's dope guy, coke guy, whatever-you-want guy. People told me I looked like him when he was younger. They even called me "Lil Butt Butt." I didn't mind. Sometimes it was good to be mistaken for a king.

I was sitting there thinking about how being a lookout didn't look so hard—I was practically doing it already—when the door opened, and in walked Pop.

2

Pop

Pop's real name was Walter Spencer, but we always called him Pop. He worked for Operation Champ, a program that brought sports equipment to kids in the projects. They had trucks that drove around making pop-up playgrounds out of empty lots. On weekends, when my mother was at work, Pop would take me all over West Baltimore with him. Sometimes we'd go to games when he was coaching at Robert C. Marshall, or we'd play tabletop games at the Greater Model Rec Center, or we'd just drive around with his friend Gurney, stopping at houses where Pop and Gurney knew people. Sometimes we'd visit Pop's mother, Miss Elma, who lived on Argyle Avenue.

"Is that where we goin'?" I asked hopefully, as we left the projects and made our way down Orleans Street. "To Miss Elma's?"

"Not today," said Pop. "We goin' somewhere else."

It was one of those October days that already feels like winter, and the wind was making my nose run. Pop held out the bottom of his sweatshirt for me to wipe across my face. As we approached the point where Orleans splits into Franklin and Mulberry, he looked down at me.

"I hear you been getting into fights at school, boy."

I didn't say nothing 'cause it was true. The day before, somebody had called me a fat bitch in the cafeteria and I had swung at him.

"Didn't I tell you not to fight unless it's self-defense? People calling you names don't mean nothing. Don't mind what they say."

"I know."

"Now if someone lay hands on you...that's a different story. But don't be the one starting it."

I nodded, concentrating on the flow of cars down St. Paul Street.

"You heard me? You ain't gonna be starting no more fights?"

"I heard you." *Until the next person call me a fat bitch.*

We rounded the corner onto Pennsylvania Avenue.

I don't know what you know about Pennsylvania Avenue now, but the Avenue of my childhood was a bustling place, lined with storefronts. The midpoint of the street was Lafayette Market, where arabbers sold fresh fruit and vegetables and you could get a box of chicken gizzards from a stall for fifty cents. Money exchanged hands at all hours of the night and day.

I always liked these trips to West Baltimore because I had family on every other block. We'd pass by at least three of my mother's sisters' houses on our way up the Avenue, and I'd run in to say what's up to my cousin Yok or go to the bathroom or get a drink of water. This was as necessary as it was entertaining; Pop wouldn't ever spend money on stuff like that.

This time around, we didn't stop but kept walking until we turned onto Laurens Street. At the corner of Laurens and Division, we went into a brick rowhome. Pop turned on the television and told me to wait in the living room. Then he disappeared into the back of the house. I sat down on the couch, knowing it would be a long wait, disappointed that it was one of these days. I know what you're thinking at this point, but even at six years old I knew what a dope fiend looked like. They had big puffy hands and track marks along their forearms. Pop didn't look like that. He was a real muscular dude.

A few hours later he emerged, looking exactly the same. Outside, the sun was beginning to go down. We walked back home along the same route, passing my Aunt Nita's house, my Aunt Loretta's house, and my Aunt Cakie's house on Pennsylvania Avenue.

That Monday after school, I was throwing a football back and forth with Shang in the courtyard when a drunk slouched against 131 building started yelling curses at us. I had seen him there a few times before, and he always yelled at me.

"Why don't that guy just leave us alone?" I called out to Shang, loud enough for the man to hear.

Shang caught the ball and held it.

"Yo, what's your name, Tater?"

"Dante Barksdale."

"What's my name?"

"Richard Barksdale."

"What's Woody's name?"

"Alvin Barksdale."

"Tater, Woody is Alvin Barksdale, *junior*. That man over there? That's Alvin Barksdale, *senior*."

That's how I found out Pop was not my father.

Then I began to hear things. I would hear Shang and Woody talking about Pop, and then I'd hear my aunts talking to my mother. *Carlene, Tater don't need to be running around with that dope fiend motherfucker.* I even heard stories about Pop killing people. That I couldn't wrap my head around. In my eyes, dope fiend or not, father or not, Pop was a man of integrity.

But our trips into West Baltimore did become less mysterious. Now when we rode around making stops with Gurney—whose puffy hands rolled the windows up and down—I knew what we were looking for. Once we got pulled over on Pennsylvania Avenue when Pop was driving, which was rare. Gurney was in the passenger seat, and I was in the back. I don't know what Pop said to the cop or what he gave him, but the cop didn't do nothing rough and we were sent on our way.

As I got older, I saw Pop less often. He would leave early in the morning and come home real late. Sometimes, my mother would send me to stay with our aunt or grandmother over Perkins projects, and I would know it was because they were fighting. He had me in his corner, but he couldn't ever get a hold on Shang or Woody. Then one morning, a few weeks after my ninth birthday, Pop left early in the morning and didn't come back.

When they first started dating, Pop gave my mother a poem that she stuck up on the wall of our apartment. The poem is called *Desiderata* and it begins like this:

> *Go placidly amid the noise and haste,*
> *and remember what peace there may be in silence.*
> *As far as possible without surrender*
> *be on good terms with all persons...*

I think I know that poem by heart by now.

3

The Barksdales

Later, I found out more about Alvin Barksdale, Senior. Apparently my father was a slick dude back in the day. Uncle Rebo told me he ran numbers for an underground lottery in the sixties and seventies. He went around collecting numbers for people in exchange money, and whichever number won, he'd deliver back the winnings. Rebo said my father dreamed of winning the lottery and getting my mother out the projects. But eventually he went crazy, either from the numbers or from seeing Moms have my little sister Quanza by Pop. Either way, he never got her out the projects. He got drunk outside her building and yelled at her kids instead.

But I did get something fatherly from Alvin without him needing to lift a finger. Something that has been a blessing and curse my whole life. Something Alvin got from his mother, my Grandma Romaine Barksdale, who gave all her children her own last name. That name was made famous by my father's cousin, Nathan Avon Barksdale, or Uncle Bodie, as I knew him. For most of my childhood, Uncle Bodie controlled the flow of heroin in and out of Lexington Terrace and Murphy Homes as a lieutenant for Melvin Williams. Everyone was afraid of him. He couldn't be destroyed by bullet or by jury; he survived more than twenty gunshots during his reign and was notorious for beating homicide charges. Until 1986, the year I turned twelve, he seemed immune from the forces that took down everyone else. Then he received a fifteen-year sentence for torturing three people on the ninth floor of the Murphy projects.

When I was in fifth grade, my history teacher asked each of us to bring in a newspaper article about a current event to share with the class. When it was my turn, I stood in front of the class and read aloud from *The Baltimore Sun* about the West side kingpin who had, once again, been found not guilty for murder. The author of that article was David Simon. People say Bodie was the inspiration for Avon Barksdale's character on *The Wire*, but let me tell you, the HBO producers got all kinds of things wrong. Stringer would never have been friends with Bodie. Marlo could never have killed him. And Omar would never have existed. A dude like that would have been dead right away.

Uncle Bodie is the reason everyone in Baltimore—cops and street dudes alike—knows my name, and *The Wire* is the reason the rest of America knows it. On the street, it works in my favor. In front of a judge, not so much.

The first time the Barksdale card worked against me was the summer after I turned five, and my mother and I walked one block over to Charles Carroll of Carrollton Elementary School to get me enrolled in kindergarten. I already knew every teacher in the school, because they'd all called my mother about Shang at one point or another. When Shang was in fourth grade, he got caught with something like 700 hundred dollars in his bookbag. A lot of money for a nine-year-old to be carrying around, especially in 1979. My mother told the principal that Shang must have stolen it from her purse. Shang's dumb ass denied it, saying he earned that money himself. Luckily, nobody believed him.

Anyway, when Moms and I got to the front office that day, the woman behind the desk asked for my name.

"Dante Barksdale," I said.

"You said Barksdale?"

"Yup."

The desk lady paused for a moment, and looked up at my

mother with a pained expression.

"Unfortunately, there's no room for Dante here," she said. "The school is overcrowded as it is. I suggest you take him to Thomas G. Hayes."

Thomas G. Hayes Elementary was across the street from Somerset projects, right behind the great and powerful Dunbar High School. To get there, I would have to leave the projects and cross Orleans Street. People were always getting hit by cars on Orleans, my aunt Valerie included, so my mother was not too happy about this arrangement. For me, the prospect of getting hit by a car wasn't nearly as bad as not attending kindergarten with all my friends from Lafayette. Instead, I would be in a classroom with little project dudes from all over the East side. Kids came to Thomas G. Hayes from Somerset, Somerset Extension, Latrobe, Deakyland, Target City, Lester Morton, all over. Remember what I said about rivalries within the projects? Well, it was even more so between them. Where you came from determined a whole lot.

Nathan Avon Barksdale (Uncle Bodie)

4

The Rules

It always went down on the way home from school. Nevermind the classrooms, the teachers, the lunch monitors—I learned the rules from Orleans Street and Central Avenue in the three blocks I walked every day.

I remember walking down Central on my way home one day when I found myself against the wall of one of the Somerset buildings, across the street from Dunbar High. Blocking my view of the high school were three boys from my class—Troy, Darnell, and Tyrone. The week before, I had won the third grade math contest (shocking everyone except my mother) and since then I'd been a pain in everyone's ass. I must've been cracking on these three during class that day, though I couldn't remember what I had said.

Troy Hill was the one got in my face. "Yeah, you scared now."

I kept my expression deadpan. "Scared shit, what's up?"

Just then around the corner came Craig Pinkney. Now, you have to understand, back in the projects I gave Craig Pinkney the blues. I used to beat him up in the big field behind 131 building for no reason except he had pretty hair. Don't get me wrong, he was my boy, but we fought a few times. So when I saw him come around the corner that day, me against a brick wall and Troy and his crew feeling vengeful, I didn't know what he'd do. Suddenly, he looked huge to me.

"Y'all niggas messing with my muthafuckin' homeboy?"

Just like that, and they ran.

That was Rule #1: Even if you beefin in the projects, you have each other's back out here.

Damon and Foo were two boys from Latrobe who used to hang around outside the candy store at Old Town Mall. They would catch little Somerset dudes on their way out and take their money *and* their candy. And the little Somerset dudes would come to school the next morning and fuss about it. One day, I decided to walk with them to the mall after school. I knew Damon and Foo wouldn't give me no trouble. I was from Lafayette projects, the biggest in the city. Rule #2: Know your place in the hierarchy.

Pockets stuffed with candy, my classmates and I emerged from Sol's and started up the brick walkway that ran through the center of Old Town Mall. I had my hands curled in fists in my pockets, ready to fight for my little bit of money, but nobody messed with us the whole way down. *Maybe they see me and that's it*, I thought. *Maybe I don't even have to do anything.* But as we rounded the corner onto Aisquith Street, we heard laughing and saw two boys coming towards us. Both wore long sleeves and jeans, even though it was September. Foo had a candy worm sticking straight out of his mouth. Damon had a good four inches on all of us.

The other boys started backing up, like they were about to take off running, but Damon and Foo were looking at me.

"Shawty, you Shang brother?" Foo asked.

"Yeah. Tater."

Damon and Foo looked at each other and Damon shook his head.

"You go head."

"What?"

"Go head. Go home, shawty!"

I wasn't about to argue. Foo was already approaching one of my classmates, who had begun shoving candy in his mouth like he could save it that way. I strolled casually away, sped up only once I was out of sight, and got back to the projects within about four minutes.

That afternoon taught me Rule #3: No one messes with Barksdales. By the time he entered middle school, Shang was carrying a .44 Bulldog pistol to school every day. His days of taking orders from Kevin and Ock were over. The two of them had gotten locked up, and in their absence, Shang had linked up with his boy Stink and become a stick-up boy. They didn't sell drugs now so much as rob the dudes who did, partly because it required less organization, and partly because they wanted the dope more than the money. I don't know when exactly Shang started sniffing, but I know it was normal back then for guys to be selling and using at the same time. Whereas now the dealers look down on the fiends, back then they were the fiends, just in gold chains and MCM sweatsuits. And when Shang got high, he was trigger-happy and conscience-free; it was good to be someone he loved. His ruthlessness guaranteed my safe passage home.

It also guaranteed that I walked home in style. At that time, the only joke people could make about me was that I wore Shang's clothes, and I didn't even care 'cause I looked fresh to death every day. This was the era of Run-D.M.C. and LL Cool J, and Shang wore whatever hip hop told him to wear. On my tenth birthday, he gave me my own pair of navy blue and white Adidas Forums with a $139.00 price tag stuck to the bottom.

Though I didn't realize it at the time, I played a key role in Shang's business. I probably carried over a thousand packages without realizing what they contained. Shang was real sneaky about it. He would hand me a backpack with some shoes hanging out and say, "Yo go put my tennis in the house." And me being little and eager to win Shang's approval, I would accept what he gave me without question.

So I was doubly protected—by my address and by my last name. If our hood was a mini-Baltimore, then Shang was a mini-Uncle Bodie.

Not long after the incident with Damon and Foo, Alvin Barksdale, Sr. paid us another visit. We were living in a low-rise behind the Exxon gas station on Fayette, and he was standing outside in his usual drunken state when Shang and I got home. He cursed at us as we walked past. This time, instead of ignoring it, Shang spun around and pushed him hard. Alvin stumbled, and then fell backwards onto the sidewalk. Shang held his arms down while I reached into Alvin's pockets. I remember exactly how much we stole from our father—36 dollars—because he was carrying one each of the four smallest bills.

I took the money and ran inside and locked the door. I could still hear him outside cursing us, and I wondered where Shang had gone. After what seemed like hours, Alvin wandered away and Shang came to the door.

"You wanna go to the store?"

We went and got ourselves some Frosted Flakes.

5

The Gas Station

From the ages of nine to thirteen, I worked at the gas station on the corner of Fayette and Central. Most of the young guys from Lafayette projects worked there at one point. For me, the motivation came from my mom's crackdown on snacks. She didn't want people to crack jokes on me so she wouldn't let me eat a lot. So I figured I would make my own money and buy what I liked.

There was a stigma attached to the gas station in the greater community, because people didn't trust us project boys. But I revolutionized that shit. First of all, everybody who came through knew who I was. And it was some celebrities in East Baltimore around that time. They either were slinging crack rock or had a wicked jumpshot, like Biggie said.

"Oh my god! Oh my god, look!" Marcus was wide-eyed and pointing at a car pulling into the station. He and his brother Dooron had just moved up here from Danville, Virginia, and you knew they were country boys by the way they got so excited. We called Marcus Willie Nelson.

We all turned. Muggsy Bogues was gliding smoothly into the empty space in front of Pump 2. Marcus was still going nuts.

"That's Muggsy Bogues, y'all!"

Mugs parked and got out of his car. He had brought the Muggsy Mobile, a 1987 Ford Fiesta for which he was the poster boy at the time. I thought of how my mom used to say that Reggie Williams had promised to buy her a car. *Better not wait on it,* I used to think to myself. We never saw Reggie again after he got drafted. But Mugs always came back.

"Sup, Lil Butt Butt," he said, strolling over to us.

"Sup, Mugs!" I said. "Man, let me pump that gas and wash your windows!" I knew he'd give me five or ten as a tip, as opposed to the singles I usually got.

"Go 'head Lil Butt Butt! But don't leave no streaks in there. Make sure you do it right."

I had learned from the gas station that being nice gets you paid more. I was in the habit of sending customers away with a little speech—"Have a nice day, don't run red lights, don't drink and drive, and buckle up!" The older folks loved it. "You stay polite just as you are!" they'd say, handing me a couple folded dollar bills.

The other reason for the gas station getting so popular was we learned how to utilize our platform. When the Lakers won the NBA championship in 1985, they sold Lakers t-shirts at the flea market for like a dollar. My boy Cee and I were over there with our homeboys Big Scooter and Mark Holmes, and Big Scooter had the idea of buying all the shirts and reselling them. He didn't have enough money on him, so he and Mark each bought about ten and told the vendor they'd come back the next day. Cee and I did happen to have the money on us, so as soon as Scooter and Mark walked away, we bought rest of the stockpile, like eighty-odd shirts. All we had to do was go back to the gas station and sell them to whoever pulled in for ten dollars a piece. Lord, we made a killing that day. Cee had a knack for the hustle; it was our loss when his mother moved their family out the projects and up the hill to Deakyland.

Another time, this lady who was working as a temp at the station showed us how to work the pumps from inside the booth. For whatever reason, this lady trusted us with that information. So after they left her in that booth for about five days with no relief, she left, and we broke in with a crowbar Crutty Mone took from his stepfather's '74 Impala. For a few hours, we ran the booth, selling people gas and keeping the money. No one even questioned it until someone's mother stopped by the station and happened to look through the window. A few days later, we heard our homeboy Eric broke into the booth to get cigarettes. After that another dude broke in after him, and another after that. Someone must've caught wind of our method and spread the word. We weren't mad about it. We just wished we'd thought of it.

Sometimes, we messed with people when there wasn't even money in it, just for our own entertainment. There was a speed bump right in front of the station on the side where Irvin's convenient was, and somehow cars never managed to slow down for it. We loved watching them catch air and then hit hard, especially the real nice ones. When a shiny silver Corvette pulled up to the intersection one day, we saw an opportunity.

"How fast that thing go?" Jerome called out to the driver from where he stood at the pump.

"Oh, what I do on this street won't do it justice!" the driver called back. He looked just barely older than us.

"Okay man, let's see it!"

The light turned green, and the driver held up one finger, like *wait there.*

Jerome turned to me and grinned. A few minutes later, we heard the Corvette roaring back down the street in the opposite direction. It must have been doing about sixty-five miles an hour by the time it got to the speed bump. I'm telling you, this Corvette went three or four feet in the air. And when it landed, there was a *screeeeech* and actual sparks flew through the air. The driver whipped his head around to look for us. We were holding up the numbers *8* and *9* from off the gas station price sign.

"I'ma *fuck* y'all up!" he screamed.

We took off into the projects. We knew no one would follow us in there. Like I said, nobody trusted the project boys.

The Lafayette boys

6

The Nice Days

When the weather was nice, Crutty Mone, Michael and I would go all the way down Caroline Street to the waterfront. Back then there was no Whole Foods, no Michael Phelps condos. Where Caroline Street and Central Avenue meets the water now, there used to just be an old abandoned building. We would pick out bricks from it to use as hammers, and then bang nails into loose planks of wood. Once we had a decent raft to float on, we'd hop into the water.[1]

One day, after about a half hour of playing in the water, Michael got antsy. He jumped off the raft and started swimming away from the dock.

"How come I'm the only one in here? Y'all scared of sharks?"

Mone and I looked at each other.

"Dare you."

Soon we were all in the water.

"I'm goin' all the way to the Bay!" Michael shouted.

"The Bay's nothing, I'm goin' to the Atlantic!" I shouted back.

A blaring horn drowned out Michael's response. None of us had noticed the white Coast Guard ship approaching.

On Saturdays, we went shopping. By this point I had

---

[1] Funny thing is, that abandoned building is now owned by the Living Classrooms Foundation, where they teach inner-city kids how to build boats.

stopped relying on Shang for hand-me-downs. I could afford my own Adidas now. We would hit Sports Mart or Charlie Rudo's or jump on the 23 bus mid-afternoon and ride out to Eastpoint Mall on the edge of the city. On the way out the mall, looking fresh as hell, we'd roll into the Horn and Horn All-You-Can-Eat Buffet. The food at Horn and Horn left you satisfied for days. They even had to-go containers. Then we'd go to the Harbor Park movie theater and spread out in the sea of squishy seats. Everywhere we went we rolled thirty deep, and whichever one of us had money would pay everybody's way.

Meanwhile, Shang's money was catching up with him. He kept getting locked up on drug charges and there was no one around to show him better. Woody had dropped out of high school during his sophomore year and gone off to Job Corps to get his G.E.D. As soon as he was eligible, he joined the army and was shipped off to Fort Knox, Kentucky for basic training.

I don't know if my mother thought the structure of military life might do Shang some good, or if she was just tired of dealing with him, but the next time Shang got arrested he was sent to the Maryland Training School for Boys. From my perspective, this was no different from him getting locked up. He would leave for a few months at a time, and then come back, get into the same shit, and get sent away again.

A few days before my fourteenth birthday, Fat Relly and Lor Herb showed up at my house looking serious.

"Yo Tater, boy!" said Fat Relly as I opened the door. "Shit just went down up in New Projects. Your brother is fucking crazy, boy!" New Projects was the new housing complex on Broadway, later known as Chapel Hill.

"Fuck ya'll niggas talkin' bout?"

"He was up there with Flyhead Mike and Tabitha"—Mike was one of Shang's homeboys, and Tabitha was his sister—"passed out on Mike's couch. I don't know what shit he was on. Valium, dope, I don't know."

"Oh yeah? What the fuck happen?"

"Mike and Tabitha was fighting with John Dunne, 'cause John Dunne took like ten dollars from Tabitha or something, and he wouldn't give it back to her."

"So what happen?"

"So Mike and Tabitha was fighting on him, and that's when Shang wakes up out of his trance and comes outside and jumps in the fight." This didn't surprise me at all.

"Then Shang go over to this car, grab this sawed-off shotgun he had stashed underneath, put it in John Dunne's face and pull the trigger. Bottom half of that dude's face is *gone*."

My thoughts went immediately to witnesses. "Who was out there? Was it a lot of people?"

"Everybody was out there, boy."

I didn't see Shang around for the next couple of days. I heard he was hiding out at his boy Freddie West's place, somewhere between Lafayette and the New Projects. Then he showed up at the house on my birthday, looking exhausted. His girlfriend Tiera had just given birth. Shang was the father of a baby girl, Tanease.

He slumped at the table in our mother's kitchen and poured himself a bowl of cereal. He looked over at where I sat on the couch, watching television.

"You know I ain't coming home for a while, right? 'Cause I shot John Dunne."

"Damn, son." I didn't know what else to say about it.

"But look in that white puff leather jacket in the closet, there's something in there for you."

I went and looked. It was three hundred dollars in the pocket.

"Yo, happy birthday," he said.

Soon after that conversation, Homicide was at the door. Within months, Shang was convicted for attempted murder and sentenced to seven years in prison.

My brother Shang (middle)

7

The Hustle

That summer, an old friend came to visit the gas station. I was wiping down a windshield with Dietrich when we heard Cee's voice behind us.

"Shit, y'all still out here Squeegeeing?"

I turned, shaking out my Squeegee onto the asphalt.

"Sup, Cee! Fuck's up with you?"

"I'm hiding out for a little while. I got a warrant out on me in Eastern district."

Deakyland was in the Eastern district, and Lafayette projects was in the Southeastern district, so as far as the cops were concerned he might as well have been in another country. Police intel back then wasn't as quick it is now.

"Boy, how much money y'all got right now?" he asked me.

"Couple hundred. How much you got, Dee?"

"Couple hundred."

"All right, all right. That's not nothing. Y'all can triple that."

At this point, I had been working at the gas station for almost four years. It had been fun at first, having a steady income and coming up with schemes to get a little extra here and there. But the truth was, I knew there were dudes getting hella cake—and they didn't have to stand outside dripping dirty car water all day.

Cee added five hundred to my and Dietrich's four and told us where we could buy an ounce of cocaine. We went straight from the gas station to 125 playground and bought some coke from Cee's girl's mother. I remember it was pink, a color I'd never seen on coke before. Over the next two days, we bagged up more than three thousand dollars from that ounce. I'm not gonna lie, the shit came easy to me. My brothers never involved me in their respective hustles, but Shang always made sure I would know what to do if the day came. As Cee's girl's mother tossed us the plastic sandwich bag with that tiny ball of pink inside, I could hear his voice in my head. *You gotta make the decision whether you want to do this or not. Aight? I ain't telling you to do this. But if you get this amount, you should make this off it. It should cost this much. Here, watch how I bag it up…*

My mother knew I was selling drugs about twenty minutes after I started. She came looking for me on 125 playground that first night and I could see it on her face.

"Tater, people saying you out here selling drugs. Tell me that ain't the situation."

I opened my mouth to respond, but she cut me off.

"You better not lie. Ms. Diane already told me. I'm not about to have another Shang and Woody, you hear me?"

That was all she said, and then she walked back to our house. Shit, it was off to the races after that.

We had the mean set up. The crew consisted of me, Cee, Dietrich, and our homies Black Man, Ronnie, Crutty Mone, and Nip. Cee was the boss, of course. At first, we stayed in the playground outside 125 building going hand and hand against Mike Tate and Fang. You had to start out in the playground as a new crew, before graduating to inside the buildings. Our product was Pee Wee Threes. For y'all don't know, cocaine used to come packed in gelatin capsules of different sizes. You had threes, twos, ones, zeroes, double zeroes, and triple zeroes. The smaller the number, the bigger the pill. So our threes was pee-wee-sized. They were five dollars when we were competing with Mike Tate and Fang, but when we made them three dollars it was over.

We spent most of our time sitting on lawn chairs in front of the building watching for police. Everyone on the block knew to look out for Melvin Russell. Or you could see Monkey Man and Doc, from the Housing Authority Police, riding in that sky blue Monte Carlo way before Denzel in *Training Day*. They were the main Police terrorizing the projects at that time. We learned to stop hustling in the playground before school let out, because there was no camouflage without the kids. The police would come down at like 11 in the morning and there we'd be, with nowhere to hide.

The first time I was arrested, I was wearing a big straw sombrero. It was hot as shit that day and I needed some shade. Melvin pulled up to the side of 130 building in his white Chevy Cavalier and found me hitting pills out of the pole on the laundry bend. He called out to his boys to lock me up. On the way to the station, he gave me some pro-bono hustling advice. "Next time," he said, "don't wear a big dumb ass hat."

After my second or third arrest, Shang and Bodie called my mother's house from Jessup, where they were serving time together. They asked her to put them through to me.

"Tater, wassup?"

"Yeah, wassup Shang."

"It's Bodie on here, too."

"Sup, Bodie."

"Tater, we hearing 'bout you getting locked up, boy. You better be careful out there."

Shang and Bodie were always telling me to be careful, but never telling me to stop.

"I know, Bodie. I will."

"You know them streets is wicked. Don't trust nobody," he added.

"You know anybody with some grams out there?" asked Shang.

"Yeah I can holla at Black Nut. He be down in 125 building with us."

"Oh yeah! Black Nut, that's my nigga. He used to be with Kennybird and us," interjected Bodie. Kennybird Jackson was one of the big dogs in the city at the time. He owned a strip club called El Dorado and I would guess he inspired the character Bird in *The Wire*.

"Tell that nigga send me some grams raw dope."

They knew it was easy to go out in the projects and find drugs. All I had to do was mention Shang and Bodie's names, and the fact that they had money, and people would practically stuff dope down my pockets. I didn't mind. Unlike in my early days of carrying Shang's "shoes" into the house, I was eating off the same plate as him now. Whatever Shang and Bodie sent back home from selling dope in prison, I would get a piece of it. Or I'd get my piece on the front end—they would tell me they needed fifty grams of raw heroin, send me the money, and I would get it cheaper than what it cost and keep the extra cash.

The money always arrived through some unknown person. Once, it was a lieutenant from the prison in Jessup who showed up at the meeting place. I couldn't believe he was the horse until he handed me a bag full of cash.

The next time Shang and Bodie called, I heard about life in Jessup.

"Yo, Tater, Bodie had to deal with this dude in the Cut." The Cut was the Maryland House of Corrections, one of the many jails in Jessup but probably the most dangerous because the C.O.'s could never lock it down.

"Damn, what happen?"

"See, Bodie was walking down the stairs and this motherfucker from PG County almost knock him over." Bodie was an amputee. When he was younger, a man ran over his leg with a car. "The dude said something like 'Get your cripple ass out the way.'"

Bodie jumped in.

"So I just smile at him. And that night, when the dude goes to bed, I go back to my bunk and use like an entire bottle of Vaseline to grease myself. Then I put my knife in mouth like a Navy seal and crawl across the floor to the other side of the dormitory. Jump in bed with that bitch ass nigga, and stab him."

"Fuck. He survive?"

"Nah."

Bodie was a ratchet dude. He and Shang were real tight, though they had different styles. Where Shang was unpredictable, Bodie was methodical. When Bodie came up with plans, he thought through every detail. He cared about results. He didn't want to get caught. This is a man suspected of killing thirty to forty people in the streets *himself,* who never had a life bid in prison. That's probably why David Simon wrote about him.

When our crew moved into the building, we traded our pills for yellow-topped and clear-topped vials, called nickels because they sold for five dollars apiece. We shared the building with Black Nut, who sold heroin in wax bags, two for ten. On the other side of the building was Tweety Bird and his lieutenant Big Peanut. They had the jumbo nickels and the double zeroes of dope.

For a while, we had the building on lock. Everyone in the crew had a job. You were either hitting, collecting money, or posted up with a gun. Usually it'd be me and Dee on the fence outside the building, looking out for police and stick-up boys and calling up to Mone and Michael in the staircase, like "Watch out for that guy in the all-black, look like his gun bulging out!" In between, we'd be calling out our product— "Yellow tops, clear tops, 3rd floor to the left"—and then calling out the rules—"Hands out your pockets, hood off your head, don't bring us no single dollar bills!" The singles took up too much space, especially the soft, crinkled bills you get from junkies. Black Man was in charge of collecting the money.

Our shop was on the third floor landing because we were still new. The more successful your shop, the higher the floor, because you needed more space in the staircase for the line. We kept our stash in the lip of the roof rather than in a separate stash house. The cops would check the roof, really feel around on it, and still come away clueless.

After the first few times getting coke from Cee's girl's ma, we started buying it in bulk from my man Reds. Reds was about the coolest dude you ever met in your life. He was twenty-two when he started giving us the work, and he drove a candy apple red 325 BMW with a droptop. You could catch Reds pulling up at 7/11 or McDonald's anytime with his top dropped, decked out in Fila apparel. He always wore this medallion with the Richie Rich logo on a solid gold rope.

One afternoon, I got off the bus after school and found Cee

and Dietrich waiting for me in front of McDonald's.

"Tater," Cee said. "Our boy Reds got some dope called Tango and Cash and they *jamming.*"

We walked over to 200 building where Reds had set up shop. His line of customers extended from the eighth floor to the bottom floor, down the hallway, and out the building. There were enough people gathered out back to fill a stadium. Reds was doing numbers. You know niggas is getting money anytime you can say "Shop closed!" and it's another hundred people in line waiting. I heard later that Reds did 47 thousand and some change that day. The only ones making more than that were the Jamaican boys in 131 building. But it was all good, because the overflow would stay in the projects, and that was money for other shops.

Our crew had a system worked out with Reds where we would pay him $7,500 for nine ounces of coke, and then he would front us another nine ounces. So we were pushing about a half a kilo in days, pilled up. We'd sell it all, cop another nine, get fronted another nine. When we wanted to cop a Mazda RX7, which cost the same as nine ounces of coke, Reds helped us out with that, too. The next time we had $7,500 ready, Cee gave it to Reds as payment for the RX7. Reds still fronted us the eighteen ounces so we could keep up our pace. It was a cycle in constant motion.

We really broke it open for young boys to be selling drugs in the projects. Before we came on the scene, the old heads ran everything; if you were young, you were just a lookout. Now this was our shit, our crew, and we ran ourselves.

But we still tried to hide the fact that we hustled from our mothers, out of respect. Like, "There go Dietrich's mother, don't hit 'em right now."

125 playground

8

The Little Red Hen

Unlike the rest of the crew, I stayed in school. I went to Edmondson High School on the West side, and to be honest, the only thing that kept me there was the chance to play on Edmondson's football team. Woody was the one who convinced me to try out. He was back home, having gotten himself locked up so that he wouldn't be assigned to Afghanistan. It was kind of ironic; Moms had sent Shang to training school to keep him out of jail, and Woody sent himself to jail to stay out of Operation Desert Storm.

"Boy you ain't get to play football since you was over-weighted for the Lafayette rec league!" We were throwing a ball around in the Big Field. "In high school there's no weight limits..."

I caught the ball and made a face at him.

"Yeah, what's your point!"

But he made a good case. I loved playing football. Plus, my cousin Garfield was already on the team and my homeboy Lil Herb from Chapel Hill would be joining us.

It turned out to be the meanest team I ever played on. We had two quarterbacks and every position was filled. Nobody played both ways. If you were on defense, you played defense. If you were on offense, you played offense. If you missed a day of practice, we all ran. It was just like in the movies.

The highlight of my football career was when we played Dunbar High and beat them 36-6 on their homecoming night. It was the first time my mother came to a game, and she brought my little sisters and everyone else she could round up from the projects. Then we beat the great and powerful Dunbar High in front of all our East side project homies.

Garfield still teased me all the time about how I never got no pussy. I told him I liked hustling and making money better. And it wasn't that I never got none, I just wasn't getting it from the girls at school. Girls at school took time—I had to go sit with them, talk to them—when I could be getting the money. But there was one girl, Lakisha Jackson, who was on the cheerleading squad. I had seen her on the sidelines during football games. My homeboy Day Day from Saratoga and Pulaski knew her from Rock Glen Middle, and she was good friends with Garfield's girlfriend, Tamika. They were the ones who got the ball rolling one day.

Tamika: Tater, do you like Kisha?

Me: Yeah, she cool.

Tamika: Well, you don't have no girlfriend and Kisha is a nice girl.

Garfield: Yo, you ain't got no girl, you may as well date her!

Me: Fine, cool. Aight.

Kisha was with it, so that day after football practice, Tamika took Kisha home in her car and I guess they talked things over. Kisha lived in Rock Glen Apartments, about five minutes from school. She was cute, but her mother and grandmother was real strict. They gave me the blues for calling their house. They'd pick up the phone and say *Kisha ain't here.* Then she would call me back, and we would talk on the phone for hours.

Kisha was a really sheltered girl. She had three older brothers, but they were going about their lives, same as mine. So we mostly just talked about the football team and her cheerleading practices.

All my teachers knew I was hustling. They would have had to have been blind not to. I showed up to school every day in a different sweatsuit, rocking the gold chains and shell-tops. On the night of the Junior Ring Dance, while everyone else showed off in their suits and tuxes, I strutted around in a pair of Reebok Revenges, a green Champion sweatsuit, a black leather jacket, and my big Herringbone chain.

My eleventh grade English teacher, Mr. Walker, always gave me a hard time about it. He would look me up and down as I walked into class and say things like, "It's gonna be a long time in the penitentiary, boy!" But he always had my back.

In January, he assigned a report on a book of our choosing.

"I know Mr. Barksdale probably hasn't had time to give his book report his all," Mr. Walker mused aloud to the class, after Janine Hamilton had presented and there was time for one more. He was absolutely right. I hadn't given the assignment a single thought.

"But I'll make him a deal. If he gives us a report tomorrow on any book, I'll give him a 99.999 percent. *Any* book, mind you." Mr. Walker never gave out one hundreds. *Nothing is perfect*, he would say.

That's how I found myself, the next morning, explaining to my classmates the plot structure of *The Little Red Hen*.

"The climax of the story is when all the animals come back and want a piece of the bread," I told them. "And the little red hen tells them no, 'cause you ain't help make it. The little red hen was merciless."

The girls who did their reports on books like *Wuthering Heights* and *Of Mice and Men* looked like they were going to cry when I got my almost-perfect score.

Edmondson football team

Junior Ring Dance

9

Chuck Norris

Joking around in class usually got me out of trouble at school, but in the projects, trouble was unavoidable. Not long after *The Little Red Hen*, I was watching the Super Bowl at my grandmother's house. She lived in one of the low-rises behind 1101 building. We called that row of houses The Condos, because they each had four bedrooms and a porch and a yard in the front and back. My grandparents' house was the only house with hedges around the yard and a rose bush. My grandfather even grew vegetables in that yard. Shit was like the country.

Anyway, I was over there watching the game and I had a bet with the dude who worked at McDonald's that the Giants would win. When they did, I said bye to my grandmother, and headed out for McDonald's.

"Where's my money?" I said as I opened the door, but then I stopped. The robber looked up from the cash register, looked straight into my eyes, and went on taking out money. Then he jumped over the counter and sprinted out the back door. Behind the counter, my homegirl Sharon was real distraught.

"Tater, he robbed us!"

"Forreal..." I said, turning back the way I came.

It wasn't thirty minutes before I heard the cops were looking for me. I sought counseling from a homeboy and he told me to go tell the police my story.

As I walked up the alley behind McDonald's, I felt a jerk on my elbow, and looked back to see Chuck Norris already cuffing me. (We called Officer Ogden Chuck Norris 'cause he looked like him.)

"Did you rob McDonald's 'bout half an hour ago?" he asked me, as if he hadn't already proceeded on the assumption that I did.

"No."

"Sharon said you were there."

"Yeah, I was there, but——"

"Get in the car."

He wasn't trying to hear nothing.

At my preliminary hearing, Sharon told the judge it wasn't me who robbed her, but I still got a stet for a year. A stet is basically when the judge says "We'll deal with this later," and they release you without saying you're guilty or innocent.

That's how it usually went. The cops would lock you up for nothing, and then the charges would get dropped eventually due to lack of evidence. It was really the bail money that made me mad, 'cause you don't get that back when they drop the charges, at least not if you go through a bondsman. I can't tell you how much of my dope money went to Baltimore bail bondsmen.

10

Tatum

June 4, 1992 was a hot ass night. Garfield, Dee, and I had been out all night hustling. The projects were shut down because someone had killed someone thought to be an undercover agent for the Feds.

The three of us were standing at the phone booth near the gas station, passing around Philly blunts. Garfield lit a new one and offered it to me.

"Yo you graduate tomorrow, we have to celebrate!"

"True," I said, taking a long drag. But they all knew that I couldn't hang late. I always went to sleep on everyone. Besides, I was high as hell already.

I told them I was going to the house for a second.

Garfield laughed. "Nigga, you ain't coming back out."

Back at the house, I fell asleep and woke up to banging on the door.

"FBI...DEA...open up! We have a warrant!"

I kept my eyes closed for a couple more seconds. I hoped I was dreaming.

When my mother let them in, they were complete gentlemen. Nothing like Baltimore City Police. They said they had a warrant for someone called Tatum. When they asked for my name, I told them it was Dante Barksdale. I knew the warrant was supposed to say Tater, but I had no idea why they'd be looking for me.

I went upstairs and into the bathroom. Through the wall, I

could hear one of them in the next room talking to Quanza and Pili.

"Is your name Tatum?" he asked Quanza.

"Do I look like a tater to you?" I heard her reply. I almost laughed. Then another one came into the bathroom, looked at me, and called out, "There's only one male here!"

They brought me downstairs. My mother was sitting on the glass table that covered my safe, her face buried in her hands. It looked like she was crying, but I knew she was trying to hide my safe from view because she figured I had drugs and guns stashed inside it. But the Feds just had body attachments—they weren't looking for anything but me.

When they brought me outside, I saw that all up and down the block they were raiding houses. I saw Fish jump out of his window. I saw Butt Butt, Garfield, Dietrich, and a couple other guys running towards Dunbar High, dodging police and Feds. I could hear Dante Eubanks standing in his door asking the Feds to come back the next day so he could graduate from high school. Dante Eubanks never touched a gun or drug in his life.

They took us down to the Southeastern district police station. I shared a holding cell with my man KK from Chapel Hill.

"Yo, they got you too!"

"Man, why we in here?"

KK didn't know either.

I spent my high school graduation in that holding cell. My mother received my diploma in my place.

11

The Trouble

You're probably wondering how I went from playing football and giving phony book reports to being under federal investigation.

See, the trouble started when Cee met this girl name Shawnda down at Bennigan's. (Bennigan's was the sports bar by the Inner Harbor that's called Power Plant Live now.) The 2 Live Crew was playing that night, so all of us was down there—me, Tweety Bird, Reds, Squeaky, Lor Herb, I'm talking the whole of Lafayette projects. We were standing outside smoking when Cee came out, talking 'bout how he just met the baddest girl in the club.

"Her name Lil Shawnda. And she got a *friend* with her. Name *Big* Shawnda."

"Her friend need somebody?" My cousin Garfield was already headed back inside.

So Cee start messing with Lil Shawnda and Garfield start messing with Big Shawnda, and they forget all about selling drugs. Which was an issue, because this was the middle of a cycle, and Cee still owed Reds money for nine ounces of cocaine.

Me, Dietrich, Crutty Mone, all of us stayed hustling every day. And Cee still came around the building, like *gimme a thousand dollars*, *gimme fifteen hundred*, every day. But he wasn't coming back to hustle. So a couple weeks go by and he ain't paid Reds.

Finally, Reds paid us a visit. He found me sitting on the steps of 125 building.

"Man, wassup with Cee?"

"Man, I don't know what's up with Cee, I been going to school."

"He owe me like fifteen thou."

"Well, he ain't ever come around, he messing with the girl!"

Reds was our homeboy and he had a whole bunch of money, so the money we owed him didn't really mean nothing to him. He was making thirty or forty thousand dollars a day selling heroin at 200 building. The coke money was money he just blew.

He looked around, scanning the playground. Then he turned back to me. "Look, I got you with the coke," he said. "I got you now."

So Reds starts hitting me with the caine. And pretty soon, Cee starts hustling again. He had messed up some of his money but he still had some left, so he copped from someone else and got back in the game.

Now Cee and I both in 125 building, but I'm working for Reds. I got the clear-topped vials, and Cee still got the yellow tops. Cee got Dietrich on his crew, and I got Garfield. (Tweety Bird fired Garfield when he stopped working to be with Big Shawnda, so he came to hustle with me.) Cee and Dietrich cop a Nissan 300 ZX. Me and Garfield cop an Audi 4000. Cee gets locked up. I stay out. In between messing with Reds, I start messing with Tweety Bird. Bird had the coke cheap as a motherfucker. I use Reds' money sometimes, cop from Bird, take Bird's money, cop from Reds. It goes so fast. We're doing nine ounces in two or three days. We have more cash than we know how to spend.

I knew Reds and them was under investigation 'cause they was doing too much. Thirty or forty thousand a day, like I said. They had lines all day long. Plus, people were going out in the projects left and right—overdosing, I mean. We didn't know what was in the dope but that shit was deadly. I once saw a homegirl die and get brought back to life in the snow outside 200 building.

The whole projects was under investigation, really. But I wasn't ever worried. I was at the bottom of the totem pole, and they only ever looked for the guys at the top.

Reds

12

Courtside

This ain't the first time I'm courtside in Baltimore City Jail. But this time it ain't a robbery charge or a drug charge. It's a whole bunch of charges. We've been indicted with the Feds.

If you want the specifics, here's what I can tell you. Reds had been indicted, along with all of us working for him, for possession of narcotics with intent to distribute. It was a federal case because Reds was partners with Squeaky, who was getting dope from a guy from New York, and *that* dope was killing people. That dope was actually Fentanyl, an opiate none of us had heard of that was fifty times stronger than heroin and lethal in tiny amounts.

Back then, you went from the station house to the district court on North Avenue. The police commissioner would give you a bail or no bail at the station, and then you would go to the district court for a bail hearing. During the hearing, bail would either be raised, lowered, or you would be released on your "own recognizance," meaning you promise in writing to show up to court.

Well, this time we had no bails. When we got over courtside, we didn't even sit in the bullpen for long. They already had cells for our whole organization on C-section. Every other time I'd been arrested, I'd gone to T-section. This was my first time in the adult block.

At the sentencing, my family and friends filled the courtroom. We had all heard that Reds got twenty-four years and Squeaky twenty-five, with no possibility of parole for either. That was more years than any of us had been alive. I did the math. Reds would be forty-seven and Squeaky would be forty-nine when they got out. I tried to calm myself down. Those were kingpin sentences. When I heard Judge John Prevas say my name, I held my breath. One year jail time, five years probation.

I let out my breath.

I could hear Quanza cursing at the judge. I could see my mother sitting very still on her bench. I remembered her pledge that first day on the 125 playground. *I will not have another Shang and Woody.*

After the trial was over, she came over to where I was sitting on the bench.

"I hope you know," she said, "I ain't ever gonna visit you."

She kept her promise. The next time I saw her was eight months later, when the Feds let me out on home monitor...

13

The Sentence

…Only for my dumb ass to be arrested again on drug charges. Station house again. Courtside again. This time I was released on bail. While out on bail, I prepared to go to prison. I knew I wouldn't get lucky twice, and I didn't.

I went back to trial, was found guilty, and received a sentence of ten years without parole by Judge John Carroll Byrnes. I had gotten my second bid before Shang did, and it was longer than any he'd served. My mother wasn't getting another Shang or Woody, after all.

After the sentencing, they sent me up to the third floor annex, where I would live until they were ready to send me to the D.O.C. for reclassification. When the corrections officer pulled up the grill to the third floor dorm, I saw my man Hank from Deakyland.

"Tater! What's up man?"

"Sup Hank."

"What they give you?"

"Shit for real. Ten no parole."

"Dammmnnnn soooooon! How the fuck you gon' do ten no pussy?"

Once I got settled into the dorm, I went into bidding mode. I called Kisha to tell her the bad news. We hadn't been together for a little while, but I knew she was living in Woodlawn somewhere and I wanted her to know what happened. Her phone was disconnected. So I called Day Day and told him instead. *Suck that shit up nigga* was his response. Day Day would be going to play football at Wydner University and I would be going to the Maryland Division of Corrections.

I was still living in the third floor dorm when my birthday rolled around a couple of weeks later. Hank called his mother and asked her to send us some grass for the occasion. She got over the jail in like twenty minutes. Hank might have stayed five minutes at the visit and then he was back in the dorm, telling me that his mother told a story about putting the grass in the seams of some clothing.

"So where the grass at?" I asked.

"My mother didn't put it in there, that's what I'm telling you."

"Yo, your mother don't have to lie to you. If she say it's there, I believe her. Otherwise she coulda just said no."

I took the clothes he was holding and sniffed them.

"Bingo!" I yelled. "Found it."

Hank got a big ass smile on his face. It was my birthday and we had hella weed. All we did that day was watch the NCAA tournament and eat peanut butter and jelly sandwiches.

A couple of days later, the administration moved Hank to the D.O.C. We put up resistance, because Hank only had six months and you needed six months and a day to go to D.O.C., but finally Hank complied.

Not long after Hank left, I got put on 23 and 1 for banking this dude in the dorm. 23 and 1 means you're let out for one hour a day and locked up for the other 23. When you're on lockup, different rules apply. For example, when the police enter your cell, you're supposed to fight back. But the first time they came into my cell, it was like ten officers in there with me, and I saw no point in fighting.

My decision did not go unnoticed. As the police were leaving my cell, I heard someone down the row yell, "Get that nigga if he don't buck!" Then, all the way from the other side of the section, I heard one of my boys from Park Heights.

"TAAATTTEERRR."

"Yeah who that!" I yelled back.

"Yooo that's Bodie's nephew Tater! Shang's lil brother!"

They left me alone after that.

14

Inside

I arrived at the Maryland Division of Corrections in the summer of 1994. It was a bleak time for the whole country. We were just getting over Rodney King, and the first thing I saw on TV when I arrived was that O.J. Simpson had been charged with his wife's murder. Along with NBA champ Sam Cassell, another gift from Dunbar High, O.J.'s face dominated the screen that summer.

While I was at the D.O.C., my mother came to let me know that she was still not going to visit me. But because I was still in the city and my cell window faced the street, I could look out and see Shang on the ground below. He would get Leon and Dee and sometimes Crutty Mone to ride dirt bikes up and down the street. They'd do wheelies and throw up peace signs, and Shang would sit on the curb, staring up at the window he thought I was in.

That was summer. When the air inside my cell got cold and the leaves began to fall, I received word that I would be transferred again. This time, I was leaving Baltimore and taking the Blue Bird to Hagerstown.

Part II

15

The Farm

As the bus pulled into the driveway at Hagerstown jail, all we could see out the window was hillbillies chewing tobacco. They greeted us in slow, drawling voices as we exited the bus.

"This here is our shit. If you obey the rules...we will have no problems."

We walked single file into the compound. As we passed Housing Unit 1, I heard someone say, "Yo, fatass, I hear you got that ten no parole."

It was my homeboy Sharrod. He was in there with my other homeboy Shawn Stewart.

"Yo, Shawn say what up!" Sharrod yelled at my back. I turned and nodded at them but didn't say nothing.

On the way to my housing unit, I saw at least four other dudes I knew from the projects. Inside the unit, I saw all my friends through the glass of the hopper section. *Gon be trouble up in here*, I thought. It was too many guys in there who knew each other like family. Since I was too old for the hopper section, they put me on mental health. The messed up thing about being on mental health is that it's easy to get in trouble, because you're interacting with crazies. Take my boy Shannon, for example. He went crazy after murdering our rapper homeboy Greg, and he looked real bad, bumps all over his face and shit. I believe he was on Thorazine.

That first morning, my celly woke me up about thirty minutes before they hit the door.

"Just so you know," he said. "You have to be out the cell as soon as they open the door because it's going to shut immediately. They don't wait for you."

I heard him, but I moved slow anyway and almost missed breakfast. And everyone knows when you first get to jail, you're starving, because you don't have your belongings yet. As I walked out the unit toward the chow hall, one of the hillbillies spit a big glob of tobacco right in front of me. I looked back at my celly, but he shook his head, like *Don't make this any worse.* So I just kept walking.

When I got to the chow hall, I saw people I knew from all over the city. My man Curly from the projects came over and greeted me. Curly was the lieutenant for the Jamaican boys in 131 building, the only ones making more money than Reds. He was talking fast, telling a familiar story.

"Yo, Black Man told on me as a prosecution witness in federal court, I had to cop out to thirty-three years…"

"Damn, son."

I looked around for my Uncle Butt and spotted him at a table with Lumpy Joe's brother, Doc. Uncle Butt fell off after moving to Cedonia, had started using and stopped making money, and had moved back to the projects. At the time he was locked up, he was living with my grandmother in the Condos.

"Tater!" he called out, motioning for me to join them. "Let me introduce you to all the OG's." One of these was my cousin Delaino, who David Simon called D'angelo in *The Wire.* I had never met him before because he was always serving time. For what, I don't know exactly, but he was tight with Bodie.

"Be careful in here, boy," Delaino said to me, going straight into advice mode. "Don't be no loudmouth. And don't trust nobody!"

"Aight," I said, nodding. I'd been hearing this from Shang for years. Just before I left for The Farm, though, Shang had reassured me. *You gon make it in jail, son, dudes gon like you, just be yourself.*

After breakfast, we went into the yard, where I saw more familiar faces. My cousin Larry Randolph was serving five no parole for an attempted murder he caught out in Cherry Hill. Fat Relly was walking across the compound wearing handcuffs and an orange segregational uniform. Every time I saw Fat Relly in Hagerstown, he was wearing that orange jumpsuit.

It took about a month, due to an outbreak of chicken pox in Housing Unit 2, but eventually I got transferred to a regular housing unit and got Uncle Butt as my cell buddy. He made the time pass quicker by telling me stories about the projects. He took me through all the beef over the years, told me who was supposed to be tough and who wasn't tough, taught me his version of history.

"So I was in 125 playgound selling 55's and 27.5's of heroin with Gary Ulman and The Jedman," he would start. "And Walter Ingram pulls up outta nowhere and asks 'Which one of y'all name Butt Butt?' So I identify myself, you know. And Walt says 'Yeah, Kennybird told me to kill you.'"

I would play along. "Why Kennybird out to kill you?"

"See, Kennybird's mob had beef with Peanut King's mob." Peanut King was an East Side player, probably one of the biggest kingpins in Baltimore history, and Kennybird's main rival. Peanut and his man Joe Dancer ran shops all over the city, but their most lucrative spot was the corner of Hoffman and Holbrook, over by Latrobe projects. Butt told me he used to hang out a lot at Hoffman and Holbrook, enough that Joe Dancer eventually recruited him to bring dope into Lafayette projects. That meant I had an uncle on both sides of that rivalry.

"Anyway, by the time I look up," Butt continued. "Gary Ulman and The Jedman are whipping out, but Walt has the playground surrounded. So we retreat into 125 building and go up to your Aunt Ollie's place."

"Shit...they follow you?"

"Yeah. No way we'd've escaped if Joe Dancer hadn't pulled up to the back of the building just then and picked us up in his Nissan 280Z."

"Damn, boy, I know y'all was happy to see Joe."

Most days we hung out in the dayroom, which had board games and a television. One day, this big country dude from the Eastern Shore was sitting in the corner of the room throwing peanuts around. As I sat watching *25 Alive*—the only channel available in Hagerstown, and the most boring station in the history of television—I felt a peanut fly past my shoulder. You can't let that shit slide in jail, so I got up to approach the dude. But before I could take a step, old man Reds A.K.A. Rogers Evans stepped in and knocked the big fella out cold. I sat back down, feeling the same mixture of confusion and relief as I had that day on the street with Damon and Foo. Far as we were from the city, that Barksdale name still served as a shield.

That's probably why it took me so long to realize how serious jail was. At first, it just seemed like an extension of my old neighborhood—all the same players, talking the same shit, getting into the same beef. East side versus West side, D.C. versus Baltimore, whatever. But then one day in the dayroom, I was watching my man Sam Scott play chess with this dude for push-ups or money or something. I heard the call for "Count time!" so I went to get my cups to fill with ice real quick. Everything seemed calmed when I walked back into the dayroom. Then, as I was filling my cups with ice, I heard someone yell behind me. I looked back to see Sam with a jailhouse knife sticking out of his neck. I stood there, unable to move, until Butt grabbed me and said, "Boy, come on. Let's go to our cell." I'll never forget how my man Sam got stabbed over a chess game.

It was Woody who pushed me to make moves. I was on the phone with him one morning and the subject of my education came up. No one had ever brought up college during my twelfth grade year; Moms was busy raising my sisters and was just glad I went to school most days. But Woody had been through the Hagerstown college program when he was an inmate, and he encouraged me to set up a meeting with the program administrator. We both knew it wasn't good to be idle in jail.

The program administrator looked me up and down when I walked in. "You trying to follow in your brother's footsteps?" he asked.

"Yeah, I guess so," I said.

"That's too bad. Because the state is suspending all funding for college in prison." He gave that a second to sink in, and then told me, "What you can do is sign up to work in the kitchen."

I went to see my counselor. She told me I couldn't take up a trade because I had more than eighteen months left until my release date. But she had another idea.

"How would you like to go to the Youth Offenders program at Patuxent Institute?"

All I knew about Patuxent Institute was that it was in Jessup, which was closer to home than Hagerstown, so I signed up. I just had to stay infraction-free until the moves began.

The next day, I was walking through the yard with a couple homeboys after playing baseball. We saw the Park Heights boys start beefing with the Old York boys, and it didn't take long for them hillbillies to put all their asses on lockup. Watching, I was glad to be where I was from. The project boys ran too deep for all that.

The night before I left for Patuxent, my homies Ronnie Hunt and Mike G stayed up with me all night in the dayroom. We were on the honor tier in Housing Unit 2, so we were allowed to stay out until 2 a.m. on weekends. All my stuff was packed and waiting out front. The C.O. had told us, me and all the other inmates headed for Patuxent, to be ready for a 4 a.m. departure.

Mike G told me some of the shit to avoid, like don't take no drugs from no older guys, 'cause they might drug you and try to get on some freak shit. Stay away from them rowdy niggas. Just do your bid, don't let your bid do you.

"And stay away from them *lames*," said Ronnie, and he

laughed and laughed.

Around 3:30 a.m., I went back to the cell to say goodbye to Uncle Butt. We had grown close during our time as cellies. Even though no one called me "Lil Butt" anymore, he had been a mentor through the first part of my jail bid, and he had some advice for me, too.

"Listen, boy. I gotta make sure you know, jail code ain't like street code."

I knew this, but I listened anyway.

"Don't be running your mouth over there, don't be disrespecting nobody. Don't call nobody no bitch, don't cuss dudes out, just lay low and be invisible."

"I know, Uncle Butt. I will."

"Just do your bid and come home. Don't get lost in this prison life."

But I had been lying low for months, feeling more and more bitter about being locked up. Patuxent was where all the young dudes ran wild, without any uncles. I assured Uncle Butt I would stay out of trouble, but all I could think was, *fuck this being good shit.*

Delaino (right), Butt Butt (middle), and me

16

Patuxent

The ride to Patuxent was like breathing fresh air after being underground. The closer we got to the city, the more excited I got to finally have some visitors. That's the thing about being locked up in Hagerstown—folks are reluctant to visit. They know the hillbilly guards will treat them bad. And you can't avoid it, because the hillbillies are always creating new rules. If you get caught masturbating, for instance, you get charged with destruction of state property. One of my homies in Hagerstown got an infraction for *reckless eyeballing* after looking at a female officer too long.

So arriving at Patuxent felt good. The first thing I noticed was that the bread in the cafeteria was soft. In Hagerstown, the bread was so hard that it would crumble as soon as you bit into your sandwich. The bread at Patuxent was nowhere near fresh, but it was still better than the Hagerstown mess. The second thing I noticed, when I finally got settled and plugged in my TV, was that we had all the channels, not just *25 Alive*. The third thing I noticed was that Patuxent had all the pretty girls working there.

Kisha and I had broken up right before I went to jail. We had been in the gym at Edmondson High, and I was sitting on the bottom bleacher, getting ready for football practice. I happened to look up and see her sitting across the gym, talking to this dude I didn't know. I watched as the dude handed her his towel, and she wiped all the sweat off his face. *Come over here a minute,* I called out to her. *You over there wiping the sweat off another man? I ain't got nothing else to say to you.* Real dramatic, like that. I hadn't heard from her or seen her since I got locked up.

My cell buddy at Patuxent was a white guy named Brian Brown. Brian seemed like your average white guy. Apparently he had driven a truck through the window of a gun shop on Harford Road and robbed the joint with a couple other guys. He had ten years no parole, just like me.

One morning, I was in our cell reading *The Holy Koran of the Moorish Science Temple of America.* It had been given to me by a dude named Mo Donnie back at The Farm, after Butt Butt suggested that I "find something to connect with" while I served my time. I had attended one church service in the jail, hoping to do just that, but after seeing dudes serving twenty years for murder run around and hug each other, I thought, *I ain't gonna be able to do this*, and dipped. Butt Butt went to the Nation of Islam services himself, but I wasn't interested in getting involved with that. So when Mo Donnie offered me his copy of *The Holy Koran*, I packed it in my bag and brought it with me.

"What's that?" I heard someone ask. I sat up on the bunk and looked down. It was Brian. I swear, if I wasn't looking straight at his face, I would've thought from his voice he was black.

"It's the Koran!" I told him.

"Man, you know that ain't Islam, right?"

"Whatchu know about Islam?" I asked.

"Whatchu mean, what I know about Islam? You think a white dude can't be Muslim?"

I just laughed.

"Come to Jummah with me on Friday, man. I'll show you."

I agreed, mostly as an excuse to get off the tier.

On Friday morning, Brian told me that I had to take a shower to purify myself before I could go to the service. It was called *ghusl*, the Arabic word for cleansing your body before you go before Allah. After I washed up, he instructed me to put on clean clothing. Then he gave me some frankincense oil, which he said had the smell of Paradise. Finally, we went to the chapel room and waited for an officer to come by and unlock the grille. The officer that came was Kelly Sinkler, my homeboy Reds' baby moms. She was cool as shit.

Inside, all the brothers were lined up by rank. The Hadith teaches that the closer you are to the imam during the service, the more blessings you will receive. During Jummah, everyone sits Indian-style on the carpet. I saw brothers offering two rakats of prayer before they sat down, but I wasn't sure how to do it right, so I just sat down. When the imam arrived, he offered two rakats and then he began the *khutbah*, the sermon.

I understood the appeal of Jummah right away. First of all, the room is quiet. Nobody's whooping and hollering and performing; everybody is quiet, cross-legged, and listening. And when you really listen to the imam, that stuff hits your soul. It makes you think about all the stuff you've done, how far from God you've been.

When the imam finished his *khutbah*, we stood as a congregation to offer two more rakats of prayer. Then the imam asked if there was anyone who felt like they wanted to commit to Allah.

For a while, I'd been thinking on how to right my wrongs. I had done some stuff, I knew, and I figured my prison bid was the time to repent and start working on my salvation. The Christian method was out of the question. I wasn't feeling *The Holy Koran of the Moorish Science Temple of America*. But as soon as the imam invoked Allah, the entirely merciful, the especially merciful Allah, I thought to myself, *this is it, this is how I save my soul.*

I agreed to take my *shahada* right then and there.

"There is No God but Allah and Muhammad is his last and final messenger," said the imam.

"There is No God but Allah and Muhammad is his last and final messenger," I repeated.

My witnesses were Brian Brown, a.k.a. Hakeem, Garnell

Carter, a.k.a. Hamza, and few other brothers. After the service was over, Brian was on my heels, telling me all the things I couldn't do anymore.

"You know you can't be cussing cause the angels gonna be writing down all the things you do," he said. "And you can't talk about people behind their back, you gotta be humble, you have to live with good Muslim *adab*." That's Arabic for the Muslim character. "And you can't eat pork anymore."

"I don't eat pork anyway, Brian," I said. I was all smiles.

Later that month, my homies Day Day and Devin from high school came to visit. Brian's baby moms came to visit him at the same time, so we walked from our tier to the visiting room together. Afterward, as we were walking back to the cell, this big dude accosted us in the hallway.

"Sup with your baby moms?" He was two inches from Brian's face. "Why she ain't with a brother?"

Brian brushed him off—"I ain't tryna fight right now"— and we kept walking.

Back at the tier, we found out the dude who accosted us was in the Nation of Islam.

"Brian, we gon' to have to deal with this dude," I told him. Never mind what Uncle Butt said, jail code means you protect your celly. If somebody disrespected Brian, he was disrespecting me.

The next day, we ran into him again on the way to the chow hall. He was still on that same bullshit about Brian's baby mother. Brian brushed him off again, and we headed into breakfast.

"Brian, the next time this dude come at you, I'mma bang him in his mouth," I said.

A few days later, we saw this same motherfucker in the hallway. This time, as soon as he opened his mouth, I went at his mouth with a right jab. He swung a haymaker that barely hit me. I scooped him off his feet and slammed him to the ground. His ass had barely made contact with the floor before the goon squad was there to take us to lockup.

Once we were in lockup together, it didn't take long for the big dude to realize who I was. Or more specifically, who I was to Bodie. Bodie was doing time for a parole violation over on the D.O.C. side of Patuxent. The dude started apologizing to me through the air vents.

"Man, I'm sorry, this is messed up. I'm sorry, man, that was my bad."

He might have apologized to me the whole three days we waited for our hearing. By the time we got in front of the hearing officers, we had come up with a story about how we was just horseplaying. That's only an infraction in prison, so we got time served on lockup, and then they sent us back to our section.

It was a Friday when we got let out, so we went straight to the chapel. A unity meeting had been scheduled with all of the Islamic communities in the jail. The big dude and I meditated together, and after that everything was cool.

But I still wasn't getting any visitors, and eventually I figured out why. When I entered the Patuxent program, they told us to write down all our family members that had ever been arrested. I had written down all the names—my mother, my father, my brothers, everybody. I didn't know we couldn't have visitors who were convicted felons. Every time Shang or Woody came to visit, they were getting turned away. So I signed out the educational program, and went over to the D.O.C. side with all the parole violators.

17

The D.O.C. Side

Now the D.O.C. side of Patuxent was live. They had all the drugs and the fun, and the under-21s were kept separate from the adult population because they knew we were ratchet.

It was mostly Baltimore guys, plus about fifty guys from elsewhere in Maryland posing as D.C. boys, and a few real D.C. boys. It was beef almost every day trying to figure out who was who.

At first, I tried to mediate. One night, we were all in the rec hall and my man Lil Charles from Biddle and Wilcox was running the phones. This dude from P.G. County wouldn't get off the phone when his time ran out, so Lil Charles grabbed the phone out his hand and hung up on him. Then all the fake ass D.C. dudes tried to buck, and all the Baltimore dudes jumped to Lil Charles' defense.

"Look y'all," I said, coming over from my seat. "We ain't doing all this lil boy shit no more. If a man has a problem with another man, y'all can go to the bathroom and square up." Luckily, it didn't have to go any further than that because the officer assigned to our tier that night was a rough motherfucker from Cherry Hill called Big T-Bird, and nobody wanted to mess with T-Bird.

But I still got caught up in it. Nothing was too small to start beefing about on the D.O.C. side. We'd be on the court playing ball, and I'd call someone a name, and then here comes Lil Moon out of nowhere, flying past me, shouting "I'm with Tater, who wants to beef?" That's how my man Lil Moon was. All he wanted to do was talk to girls on the phone, play basketball, and beef. His buddy Mo, who I knew as Germo from Murphy Homes, was the same way. If I tried to make peace before a fight broke out, I'd hear Mo shouting "Fuck that, Fats! We ain't going to be keep squashing beefs!"

One time I sent this dude named DooDoo from Edmondson Village on a visit to get me some blow. He returned empty-handed, trying to tell me that he had swallowed all the smack and couldn't get it back. I didn't believe him, and after some back and forth he handed over a couple of grams. Everybody wanted to smash him, *just give us the word*, they kept saying. But that dope didn't mean anything to me, so I just chalked it up as a loss.

Another time I stepped to a couple Program dudes because they were using the court during our gym time. The one who tried to buck was my boy Big Duke from Flag House. I knew who he was right away. Big Duke committed the first murder that I ever eye-witnessed. It was 1986, in front of 131 building. He shot and killed the homie Kenny from up the hill.

"That shit was traumatic, man!" I told him, after the rest of the Program dudes vacated the court and we got to talking.

"Shit, I'm traumatized myself," he said. "I was high off crack cocaine. I killed that boy for nothing."

I had been on the D.O.C. side for some time when I ran into my OG homie Slim Nell in the chow hall. Slim Nell was Reggie Williams' uncle. He had just gotten locked up on a parole violation. As we were sitting there chopping it up, he told me about everything going on uptown.

"I have something bad to tell you, Tater," he said finally.

I knew that meant somebody been killed.

"Your uncle Butt Butt. Some lil dude up on Patterson Park shot him in the back."

My first thought was that Butt Butt couldn't have died—he always *almost* died. He always seemed to get saved at the last second, thanks to the loyalties he maintained throughout his life. To Peanut King and Joe Dancer, to his main man Bill, to Lafayette projects. Slim Nell told me a couple dudes from the projects had been in Patterson Park the day Butt Butt was killed, but no one had stepped in this time.

I thought about Butt riding around the projects in his sheepskin hat and coat, behind the wheel of a 1984 Ford Bronco II, the first SUV I ever saw. I thought about his advice to lay low, keep quiet, and get home.

I would hear later that at his funeral, the line of cars stretched from March's Funeral Home all the way to the North Avenue Cemetery. People had to get out and walk from the funeral home to the graveyard.

Slim Nell had more bad news for me. He told me that he was sorry I had lost my grandmother. This was puzzling, because I had just talked to Grandma Betty a couple weeks earlier. I said peace to Slim Nell and went to call my brother Woody.

"Yo, why you ain't tell me Betty was dead?"

"Naw, Tater, Betty ain't dead. Slim Nell was talkin' bout Grandma Romaine." My father's mother. The Godmother of the Barksdales.

"Well, why the fuck didn't anyone tell me that?!"

"I'm sorry, man. I didn't want you to be so upset that you would do something to yourself."

I told Woody thanks, but I needed to know.

As it turned out, Grandma Romaine was more of a gangster than I knew. Bodie told me later that she had spent time at WCI-J, the women's prison in Jessup. Apparently my granny was a madam, the type that wouldn't hesitate to beat you up if you crossed her.

"Your granny went hard in these streets, boy," Bodie would say proudly. "Nobody played with my aunt Romaine."

In my early childhood years, and especially in the months before Pop left, I used to get sent over to Perkins projects to stay with Grandma Romaine all the time. I loved staying with her; I was her youngest grandbaby and the only person in the world she wouldn't cuss out. Just outside her house, there was an abandoned car that I would sit in with my homie **BK** who lived in the next court. We would be in there for hours, pretending that it was our whip, that we were ballers, that we could drive anywhere. Rest in peace to Grandma Romaine, rest in peace to Uncle Butt, and rest in peace to **BK**.

Uncle Butt (middle) with Bill (right) and
Muggsy Bogues (left)

18

The News

In those days, I talked to Leon and Dee on the phone pretty regularly. They were still hustling in the projects, running their own crews now. Both of them had dropped out of Lombard Middle. Dietrich had Squeaky and Shanita, his little brother and sister, to think about, and Leon had some younger siblings to care for, too.

One day, they gave me the news that would change everything. There were rumors going around that the city was planning to demolish Lafayette projects.

"*What?*"

"I know, man!"

"How they gon' get rid of six eleven-story buildings *and* the low-rise houses? That's like 900 families!"

"I know, man!"

I could hear Dietrich cursing in the background. Then I remembered something.

"You know, my moms told me this would happen. Like years ago. She said the city and Hopkins had a plan, that they were gon' knock down Old Town Mall, and then knock down all our buildings. So that they could spread themselves out."

"Well, look like she was right."

"Nah. Them buildings too big to knock all the way down."

Leon let out a breath. "Guess we'll see."

A few weeks later, I called again. A chain link fence had gone up around the buildings. It was announced that all residents were to move out by the beginning of the summer. Most would get Section 8 vouchers for public housing, meaning they could move to another housing project. A lot of families would end up in Douglass projects, or in Somerset, or Latrobe. My mother wouldn't qualify for Section 8 housing, seeing as she had sons who were incarcerated, so she would have to find someplace she could afford to rent.

From across the fence in the low-rises, Leon and Dietrich and the others kept watch all summer as the workmen dismantled our buildings.

"They takin' out the refrigerators, man! We see 'em!"

"They takin' the fences off the buildings!"

"They gettin' all the windows out next!"

In the middle of August, I called Leon when I was in the dayroom alone.

"What's happening now?" I asked.

"I think they really doin' it, Tater. They really about to knock our projects down."

Then he got real quiet, and I could tell that he was crying.

Around noon on August 19, 1995, I got a knock on my cell door. It was Ms. Danzler, one of the correctional officers in the jail and a relative of mine on Bodie's mother's side.

"Tater, you wanna watch your projects go down on the big TV?" She meant the television in the dayroom. We weren't supposed to leave our cells during count time, but she gestured for me to come.

The only other people in the dayroom were the working men. I sat down at the table in front of the television and switched the channel to WBAL. On screen was a grainy photograph of Lafayette projects when they first opened, in 1955.

I tried to remember what I knew about the projects' beginnings. My mother was real young in 1955, living with relatives in New York. She had been sent away after getting bitten by a rat in my grandmother's apartment, and when she returned, my grandmother was living in one of the new high-rises. This was during a period called "slum clearance," when the Housing Authority of Baltimore City was trying to concentrate the city's black population downtown. They advertised the high-rises as being clean and rodent-free, with push-button elevators and ceramic-tiled floors. Those giant buildings scared her, my mother told me later. But she stayed, because she was home, and some years later the projects became home to me, too.

I remembered coming home from kindergarten to find our apartment filled with cameramen. My mother was sitting on the couch, spine straighter than usual, with her legs crossed and her hands on her lap. Someone had a bright light trained on her, and someone else was holding what looked like a giant Frisbee covered in tinfoil. A well-dressed man sat beside her. My mother was in the middle of saying something when I walked in.

"Yes, this is how it's always been. Here's my baby, you can ask him..." She motioned for me to come sit next to her.

The well-dressed man looked down at me and gave me a cheesy grin.

"How you doin', little man?"

"Good."

"Tell me, have you lived here in Lafayette projects your whole life?"

I nodded.

"Do you think it's a good place to live?"

I looked at my mother. She squeezed my hand and said nothing.

"The elevator smells like piss," I said.

The man laughed.

"Carlene, let's talk about your work on the tenant council."

The next morning at school, my teacher had come over to my desk, put her hands on either side of my face, and beamed at me.

"You know you're a TV star, Dante?"

"Huh?" I asked.

"You were on TV last night! Didn't you see it?"

As it turned out, the well-dressed man in my house had been Richard Sher, co-host of the show "People Are Talking," which ran from the late 1970s to mid-1980s. The show is famous now for launching Oprah Winfrey, who spent the first six years of her talk show career alongside Richard Sher. That afternoon, they were filming an expose on the conditions of public housing in Baltimore. It's too bad all this happened before YouTube; I never did get to see my television debut.

The broadcast returned to the present moment. Crowds had gathered along Orleans Street to witness the explosions. It looked like a giant block party, stretching from Dunbar High to Old Town Mall. I read later that more than 30,000 people came out to watch. Traffic stopped along the Jones Falls Expressway. People were leaning out of their office windows to get a better view.

And then, clouds of white smoke covered everything. The camera crew must have been somewhere on Baltimore Street, because 125 building was the one I could see, leaning, leaning, falling, gone. That would be the image in the newspapers the next day—125 building, half there, half nowhere. I had spent most of my adolescence in that building's stairwell. It was the scene of all my crimes, the reason I had years left in my sentence. And now it was dust.

When the smoke finally cleared, the ground was flat. The whole thing had taken about twenty seconds. I felt lost all of a sudden, disoriented. My sense of belonging in the world felt shaky for the first time. Where was I gonna hang at now? Where would Leon and them go? Would they be safe in Douglass, or down Perkins, would they be safe over Somerset?

And what about the six parties bumping in the projects at any one time? I remembered partying in 131 building, and then going over 200 building and finding a hundred people on the third floor, and a hundred more on the seventh. During the day, it was two thousand of us outside at all times. Go into any housing project and start counting people, it's two thousand people outside. It might not look like it, but you got twenty people in that pocket, forty over there, twenty more standing around there. And in every apartment, you had the tenant and her sister in there, and all their cousins from other neighborhoods visiting. It was always noisy in the projects, like living in a stadium. Where would all the noise go?

I wasn't about to let Ms. Danzler see my face. She had come up behind me and we watched together as the dust settled and the crowds cheered.

"They knocked down your projects, boy!" she teased. "Where you from now?"

I kept my eyes on the television. "You know they gon' knock Lexington Terrace down next."

She had no response for that.

Slim Nell was gone by that point, so none of my Lafayette homies was really around to rap to about what happened. And Ms. Danzler wasn't the only one to give me the blues. The next time I was on the basketball court and I let out my usual victory cry of "Lafayette projects!" after hitting the shot, dudes came back at me, like, "Where's that at? That shit gone!"

Not that it was any consolation, but I turned out to be right about Lexington Terrace. They knocked it down the next year, in 1996. In 1999, they came back and got Murphy Homes. Then they went and got Flag House. And in 2001, they knocked down the building on Broadway and Orleans where Shang shot John Dunne in his face.

Every demolition was like a cup of water tipping over, the way communities spilled into each other. People went from Lafayette to Douglass or Somerset, from Flag House to McElderry Park or Highlandtown. And of course that started beef. I swear on my life, this city wasn't as violent before they knocked down all our projects and mixed the cultures up. There's a difference between knowing each other from the womb and knowing each other from the corner.

Growing up, I didn't have friends being killed in the projects. We used to hear about murder, and sometimes we would see a murder happen, but it was always an outsider coming in and getting killed. In our culture, we fought all the time, but we never tried to kill each other. And dudes from other neighborhoods didn't try, either, 'cause shit, who wants to beef with two thousand dudes?

So it was a new phenomenon for me when, after they knocked down our buildings, I would hear in prison about some of my boys getting killed or killing someone and getting life. These were the same boys who had run to help when the old ladies pulled up with grocery bags, who had put in twenty dollars apiece when someone's lights were about to get cut off, who had called out to their homeboys late at night, *Yo turn your car music down, people asleep!*

19

Jessup

Three months before I arrived at MCI-Jessup, the governor of Maryland announced that he would never approve parole for prisoners serving life sentences. This became known as Glendenning's "life means life" policy, justified by the story of Rodney Stokes, a lifer who went and murdered his girlfriend while out on work release. Before, getting a life sentence meant you were gonna be in prison for a long, long time. Now, having a life sentence meant you were gonna die in prison.

My first cell buddy at Jessup was one of the lifers whose sentence became literal after Glendenning's announcement.[2] Joe was already an old man, and the news made him go crazy. He stayed in our cell fighting demons all day. But let me tell you, this old man Joe had all the dope in the jail. Within a few days of sharing a cell with him, he had taught me all the OG code words. "Harry don't hold," for example, means don't

---

[2] Eventually, Joe did get released, along with 130 others, as the result of a case called *Unger v. Maryland*. They're known as "the Ungers" now, and they have meetings every Monday and big parties every year out in Carroll Park. It's real nice. And you know what's funny? The ones that really didn't do the murder, they'll tell you, and the ones that really did do it, they'll tell you, 'cause they don't got nothing to lose now. So many of them were locked up for *nothing*, but they're just happy to be home, most of them.

bring any contraband into the cell. One day, I looked down from the top bunk and saw he had about fifteen fingers on the locker. Fingers are about ten grams of heroin compressed into finger-looking objects—and he had fifteen of them. *Okay,* I thought to myself, *looking like this old man is crazy...with 150 grams of raw smack in the cell.* He must've been making stacks. But then, it was Jessup, drugs were plentiful, and there were plenty of dope boys to go around.

Joe and I made our cell into Caesar's Palace. We started out with a bunk, two metal lockers, a toilet, and a whole bunch of navy blue towels. I had been collecting the prison towels for a while, so I had probably forty of them.[3] First, we hung a string from the wall and draped towels over it to make a curtain in front of the toilet. I put one of the metal drawers from my locker over the space between the string and the wall, so it was like a little bathroom. Then I broke down a bunch of cardboard boxes into squares, wrapped towels around the squares, covered each square with plastic from the trash bags, and laid them down on the floor like wall-to-wall carpet. Joe and I made a dresser by stacking the rest of the drawers, and I put my TV on top. As a final touch, we twisted some toilet paper real tight, dipped one end into oil, and lit it—jailhouse incense. When you know you gonna be someplace for years, you gotta make yourself comfortable.

My first couple years at Jessup, I worked in the kitchen with my homeboy Herb Garrett, who we called Big Herb because this nigga's muscles had muscles. Dude looked like Hercules. Big Herb grew up in Lafayette projects, and later moved to Greenmount Avenue. He graduated from Edmondson before I got there, but I knew who he was 'cause he was one of those

---

[3] You could usually trade two cigarettes for someone's towel. A whole pack was worth about hundred dollars, which is probably why so many C.O.'s snuck in packs with them.

dudes people talked about.

Big Herb and I were in charge of bringing the food cart to the guys on lockup. Feeding lockup was no easy task, and they wouldn't let no anyone feed them. These were the dudes who disregarded all the rules, who had stabbed somebody in the jail, or busted someone's head open, or thrown something at the police. They would take these baby powder bottles, the ones with the holes in the lid, and fill them with feces and urine and spoiled milk and dead mice and whatever else they could find, and shake them up. Shit bottles, they were called, and they weren't just for decoration.

So it went without saying that me and Big Herb would deliver messages and packages from guys on the outside. The way the food trays were stacked on the cart, you could hide a bag of cookies or a bag of heroin in, say, the third one from the bottom. Mind you, I got paid for my deliveries—a cookie here, a nug there. Rarely would the C.O.'s search every single tray, but I had to assess the situation carefully. Some days, I'd have to tell them, "Yo, I ain't gonna do this, McCullough working today!" If Ike or Lee was down there, though, it was chill. All they wanted y'all to do was not start fights or fires or throw shit. I would even hear Ike call out "Shop open!" when I came down, the way you hear drugs being sold in the street.

I visited lockup a few times myself while working lockup. The first time—let me tell you how stupid the reason was. Me and this dude Lil Vice were working the table for a basketball game, D.C. versus Baltimore. He was doing the books and I was doing the clock and the score. At a certain point in the game, two of our homeboys got to fussing on the court.

"Man, you need to just stop and play basketball!" I called out to Lil Vice's homeboy, who had clearly been in the wrong.

Lil Vice turned to me. "Shut up, man, you ain't got nothing to do with that!"

"You ain't see that?" I said to him. "He just fouled the shit out of that man!"

"He ain't foul him that hard," Vice snapped back. "You keep

running your mouth and we can go in the bathroom."

"Whatchu mean? You wanna fight? Let's go to the bathroom!"

We went to the bathroom and tussled for a while before the goon squad came to break us up. Lil Vice thought the fight was over because the officers were there, so right before they cuffed us I popped him in the eye once more. A cheap shot, I know, but there are no rules to fighting. Lil Vice was a tough little thing—they say he killed someone—but in jail, you check the guns at the door, so you gotta know how to fight. Besides, he was from D.C., and they're supposed to love to box. Doesn't the boxing ref always say, protect yourself at all times?

Anyway, once we got to the adjustment hearing, I tried to make things quick. Adjustment hearings are set up like a courtroom, with the adjustment officer as the judge. Each inmate has a jailhouse lawyer and the state is represented by a hearing officer. "Look, I was wrong," I said to the adjustment officer. "Just send him back. I banged him in his eye." This was obvious to everyone in the room. Lil Vice's eye was the size of a golf ball. I wound up getting six months on lockup.

Can you imagine being in that little ass cell for 180 days? Twenty-three hours out of the day, all we could do was count push-ups and jumping jacks, or play pinochle with smuggled cards. Sometimes Lee and Ike would allow Scrabble. But we got shook down every morning, so we had to shove everything under the bunk and just pray for a C.O. who didn't care.

And we *might* get out for one hour a day. I say might, because sometimes it would be like 12:46 p.m. when they rounded us back up. That's when fights would break out with the police, 'cause dudes would want their whole hour. That's when the shit bottles came out. And then the whole tier would smell terrible. You just had to plug your door up, and keep lighting incense.

But lockup wasn't always the worst place to be. We had all kinds of services in there. On Fridays, my man ToeJoe from Lafayette projects would hold a Jummah service, and everyone on the tier would be silent, just like when the Christian brothers had their church service.

My celly the first time around was a D.C. dude named Terry, and his main man Pepe managed to get himself an infraction so he could come join us. Pepe planned that shit out, arriving with three ounces of weed so we could smoke the whole lockup time away. And my man Noah Walston, a.k.a. Fat Man, hooked us up with the snacks. When you're on lockup, you can't buy food from the commissary, so you need some good dudes out in population. Fat Man had 38 years, so he wasn't going anywhere. He had me the entire lockup time.

While I was on lockup, the system made some changes and brought some inmates from the D.O.C. side of Patuxent over to Jessup. As you can probably guess, that turned into a rivalry right away. One of the little dudes from Patuxent was on lockup with us, and he had a TV in his cell. This was during the NBA playoffs, when the Washington Bullets was giving the great Michael Jordan some trouble, so dudes started pressuring the little Patuxent dude to position his TV screen towards the slot in his cell so we could watch. Mind you, I never asked this dude to do anything; I merely reaped the benefits of watching.

A few days after I got off lockup, this little dude pulled a knife on me between the F and E buildings as I was walking to Jummah service. It was a big ass knife, but I just pushed him away and kept walking. Behind me, I heard someone say, "Youngin', you shoulda just put that knife in that nigga." I looked back and saw this smooth-faced dude next to the little dude, staring me down. Still I kept walking. At the entrance of the chapel, I spotted my homie Warren Clayton.

"Oh, that was *you* beefing with Howard Rice!" he said to me.

"Who's Howard Rice?" I asked.

"The dude you was just beefing with!"

By the time the service ended, it had spread all over the jail that I was beefing with Howard Rice, who I guess felt protective of the young dude from Patuxent, who felt as though we leaned on him on lockup by letting us watch his TV. This is the shit you get into in jail.

That night, an icepick made its way under the door of my cell.

"I'm telling you, don't sleep on these guys, Tater," I heard ToeJoe whisper outside. Into my mind jumped a picture of Bodie, greasing himself up with Vaseline, slithering across a jail cell floor, and stabbing someone to death in the middle of the night.

The next day, I ran into Howard Rice on the way to dinner. Bizarrely, he smiled at me.

"I knew it was something special about you," he said to me. "When you pushed big youngin' off you with that knife and got out of there. But I didn't know Bodie was your uncle."

And that was the end of our beef.

20

The Return

Late in the summer of 1996, about three years into my prison bid, my celly Lil Teddy brought our mail into the cell and handed me a letter.

"Who's Lakisha?" he asked.

I hadn't heard from Kisha since I was courtside. But this letter was long, updating me on everything that had happened to her since we'd last seen each other. She had a three-year-old daughter now, named India. She didn't mention India's father. She asked me to add her name to my visitor's list.

Just three days later, they called my name—"Barksdale, visit!"—and here come Kisha walking into the visitors' room with a big cheesy grin on her face. Behind her was a little girl with two puffs of hair on her head and a black furry jacket.

"Say hi, India," said Kisha, pulling her forward.

"Hey, India," I said, still trying to process the woman and child in front of me.

We sat down across from each other at one of the tables. I didn't know what to say, and I must have looked that way, because Kisha dove straight in.

"You know what, Tater? I was thinking 'bout you. You was like my nicest boyfriend."

"Oh yeah?"

"Yeah. I was thinking about it. You don't have no kids, right?"

"Not that I know of," I said, joking with her.

We both looked over at India, who was standing on her chair, poised to jump.

Kisha looked back at me. "She one of them terrible threes."

"Ain't it sposed to be terrible twos? She sposed to be out of that by now!"

India reached over the table and tried to swing at me. I laughed.

"Oh yeah, she bad."

Looking back, I realize what I represented to Kisha in that moment. I found out later what I had already guessed, that India's father had treated them badly and left Kisha traumatized. He was the boy she crossed me for when we broke up in high school. I remembered seeing them together at that club Hammerjack's before I got locked up, and even then he looked capable of hurting her. He had on them parachute pants and he was a dancer. But me, I was in jail, I didn't have any kids, and my credit wasn't fucked up. I think Kisha did what she had to do.

Once Kisha started coming to visit, she didn't stop. We would sit in the visiting room and talk, and usually she'd have brought me something. Since you can't have money in jail, I'd ask Kisha to go down to the projects for me, and then I'd call Leon, Dietrich, Tank or somebody and say, "Kisha gonna come pick up two hundred dollars." She really became my M.V.P.

That year something else returned to me that I hadn't seen since high school. At Jessup, I got to play football for the first time since getting locked up. And I was on the baddest team in the jail. All the other teams were segregated by region, like the East Baltimore team or the D.C. team, because people just wanted to play with their friends. But when a whole team is friends, nothing is organized, and they end up cussing each other out all game. Me, I wanted to win. So I joined a team of dudes from all over—we only had football in common. We called ourselves the MCIJ Raiders.

MCIJ RAIDERS (1996-1997)

Name	From	Position
Big Corey	Forrest Creek (P.G. County)	Offense
Paul	Forrest Creek (P.G. County)	Offense
Tater	Lafayette projects	Offense
Big Herb	Greenmount Ave.	Offense
Big Mike	Lafayette projects	Offense
Fat Man	Up the hill	Wide receiver
Treadwell	Down the hill	Corner back
Tony	D.C.	QB
Skinny Dorsey a.k.a. Dope Fiend Dorsey	East Baltimore	QB
Lil Larry Johnson	Hartford Rd.	Running back
Curtis	Lexington Terrace	Running back
Ricky Young	Lexington Terrace	Running back
Big Terry	D.C.	Defense
Pepe	D.C.	Defense
Michael Yoyo	East Baltimore	Defense

I taught the team all the plays and chants I could remember from my Edmondson days. But playing for MCIJ made Edmondson seem like summer camp, 'cause you risked tweaking an ankle with every step on that frozen prison yard field. My first year, we lost in the playoffs to the old penitentiary dudes, Tubby and Wayne Brewton and them. After that, we messed around and won three championships in a row. I remember when we beat the D.C. team (called the Redskins, of course) and I could hear Uncle Bodie on the sidelines, talking shit to anyone who would listen. *Yeah Nephew! I see you, Nephew!* He always froze his ass off in the stands during our games.

The Raiders had a song we'd sing as we entered the chow hall, victorious on a Saturday or Sunday morning. It was a chant I picked up from my man Stanley Pittman from Murphy Homes, and it went like this:

> *Down by the river / Took a lil walk*
> *Met up with the Redskins / Had a lil talk*
> *Threw them in the river / Hung them on the line*
> *We can beat the Redskins / Any ole time!*

At the end of the season, there would be a big sports banquet to award the championship trophy. Everyone was allowed to bring a visitor and it went on for hours, starting with dinner around five o'clock. They would have pizza, French fries, fried chicken, juice, everything. This dude Tyree provided the entertainment—this boy was truly blessed with talent. He could rap, sing, do comedy, you name it. He had this character he called Mophead, which involved him putting a mop on his head and walking around with his arms bent at the elbow and his wrists limp. Then the DJ would take over.

Now, the C.O.'s wouldn't realize it, but the dudes in charge of setting up the cafeteria would have snuck in a few tables from the library for the banquet. The regular cafeteria tables had bars between the legs, so you couldn't crawl underneath them. But with a long tablecloth thrown over it, a library table could serve as a miniature hotel room for dudes and their girlfriends. Everyone took turns going under. Everyone except me, that is—Kisha wouldn't give me none if it meant crawling on the floor.

At last, they would call our names, and the MCIJ Raiders would strut to the front of the room to receive our trophy. And you know we sang our song the whole way up.

Prison friends (MCI-Jessup)

21

The Brotherhood

One day, I was sitting in my cell and I saw something strange through the window. A tan Chevrolet Caprice pulled into the prison parking lot and out of it stepped John Cason.[4] This wasn't strange in itself; John Cason, or YahYah as we knew him, was the Islamic coordinator for the Jessup region, so he visited us periodically at MCIJ. But I watched as he just breezed through security, which normally took forever at the front gate. Once through, he made his way to a cell down the hall from mine that belonged to Leon Faruq. Leon Faruq was a D.C. dude with a life sentence. He was the imam at MCIJ.

At YahYah's request, the guards opened Faruq's door. YahYah entered, and a few minutes later, came back out with Faruq. The two walked outside to the front of the housing unit, sat down together on the steps, and began to talk. Meanwhile, it was count time in the housing unit, meaning *everyone* returns to their cell to be counted. I looked outside to where YahYah and Faruq were deep in discussion, and I didn't see no C.O.'s coming to fetch Faruq.

So I had it in my mind that Faruq and YahYah must be hustling. YahYah was bringing Faruq the contraband, which was how he got through security so quick, and Faruq was bribing officers with the money he made, which was how he

---

[4] Father of soon-to-be world boxing champion Hasim Rahman.

got exempted from count time.

After that day, I started watching Faruq closely. I noticed that he almost always had his door open, and that the guards seemed to mostly leave him alone. I also noticed that he never cursed or even got upset with anyone. Whenever I saw him, he was just calmly chewing on a toothpick. But if a Muslim brother borrowed money or got some dope from somebody— 'cause you know they be getting high, too—and didn't pay up, Faruq would take him aside and call his ass out. Or if a Muslim brother wanted to bust someone's head 'cause *he* wasn't getting paid back, Faruq would remind him that usury is against Islam. And these brothers listened. So Faruq decreased the level of conflict in the jail, and I found myself gaining respect for him.

One day, as I was passing Faruq's cell on the way to dinner, I heard him call my name.

"Can I talk to you for a minute?" he asked.

I stood in his doorway, which had been left open. I saw that there was no television in his cell, and no radio—it was just books, all over the place, on every surface. Faruq was sitting on his bed, leaned forward with his elbows on his knees.

"Come in," he said, waving the air in front of him.

I walked in and sat down on the dresser. "What's up, Faruq?"

"I notice something about you," he said. "You got influence in here, you know? Over the younger guys."

I hadn't realized Faruq had been keeping an eye on me, too. But it was true. If one of the little dudes did something messed up, and I said, "Yo, man, that's messed up," the little dude would listen to me.

"Yeah, most of them know me," I said, unsure of where this was going. I still wasn't convinced he wasn't hustling.

"You ever thought about being on the inmate council?"

The inmate councilors were the dudes elected by their tier to act as a liaison between the inmates and the administration. They reported complaints, put in requests for more toilet paper or more cleaning supplies, ran the phones, and helped organize the sports banquets and Family Day functions. The last inmate councilor for D building had been kicked out for selling dope or something. Sometimes the police just came and put you out the jail. In any event, D building needed a new one.

"I hadn't ever thought about it, but it seems like something I could do," I said.

Faruq nodded. "I think you'd be good at it."

He continued to look at me.

"Cool, cool. I'ma head to dinner," I said, rising from the dresser.

"Before you go—" he reached for a stack of books on the floor, and handed me a one from the top. It was a paperback, dark red, with gold letters reading *Tajweed Rules of the Qur'an.*

"If you ever want to join our weekly classes," he told me, "you'd be welcome."

I took the book, thanked him, and headed out.

Next thing I knew, Faruq was going around to every cell on the tier, asking dudes to vote for me for inmate councilor. When it came time for the election, I won by a landslide.

After that, I started going to Faruq's Arabic classes. He explained the system to me—each week, you had to pass a test on the material to go on to the next level. First you learned the Arabic letters. Then you had to learn the letters in their beginning, middle, and end forms, because the letters all connect in Arabic. In the next class, you learned the Al-Fatiha, which is the first chapter of the Quran and how Islamic services always start. *In the name of Allah, most gracious, most merciful...* And you worked your way up to the Prophet Muhammad's final *khutbah,* the last sermon he delivered from Mecca.

For me, learning how to read Arabic with Faruq meant unlearning what Hamza had taught me at Patuxent. Hamza had explained the ideas behind Islam to me, the principles and the history, but he didn't know Arabic for real at that time. This meant we had to rely on transliteration, which is when you put Arabic words into English letters. Often it makes you pronounce the words wrong, because one English letter might have four different pronunciations in Arabic. *Sirat*, for example, meaning "the straight path," is pronounced with a hard *s* sound, but you wouldn't know for sure just from the letter *s*— some Arabic letters have different *s* sounds.

Still, I flew through those classes in less than a month. Somehow the language came easy to me, like I had been hearing it all my life. One week, I finished the day's lesson and passed the test before the two hours were up, so I just went on to the next lesson. My Muslim brother Pete was amazed. But I prayed for it to happen that way. *Please let me learn this,* I whispered to Allah.

Once I finished the language classes, I was invited to a Saturday class taught by YahYah, with all of the top sheikhs in Jessup. It was a Muslim dream team in there: YahYah, Faruq, Mateen, Peter-Allen, Hakeem, Fareed, Haleem, Farruquan, Yusef, Tareef, and myself, Talib. That was the name Faruq gave me. All those dudes were older, and a lot of them had life. Brother Yusef, for example, had come home one night and found his wife in bed with another man, so he shot him and got a life sentence. This was in the 1970s. The courts were fucked up; the world, too.

In YahYah's class, we learned to recite Arabic at a high level and studied passages from the Qur'an in depth. By the second month, I was reciting Surah Al-Muzzammil, the 73rd chapter of the Qur'an and one of the longest. It asks the reader to pray for the whole night, and if he can't pray for the whole night, then for half the night, and if not half the night, a quarter of the night. But stand, it says, and break your rest in the name of God. No one could ever get through a whole verse in that class, 'cause YahYah would stop us to correct our pronunciation all the time. But it worked—I'll never say the word *qul* wrong again.

Meanwhile, another type of brotherhood was growing within the jail. The Black Guerrilla Family, or the BGF, was founded by George Jackson while he was locked up in San Quentin during the Black Power Movement. In the mid-90s, a big homeboy called Uncle Ray arrived at Jessup from California and started a Maryland chapter.

The BGF's constitution is all about black power and being conscious. It's about protecting your brothers in prison from the prison administration. All good stuff in theory. In practice, though, most of the recruits couldn't even read the chapter's constitution. They learned the structure and the rules, and left behind all the good ideas. So it went from brotherhood and uplift to organized crime.

To me, the BGF had just become another prison gang. Once I heard they were building at Jessup, I tried to make sure all my homeboys stayed away. I made a point to tell everyone in the yard to come to Jummah on Fridays.

Not surprisingly, Bodie rose quickly in the ranks of the BGF and started pressuring me to join. He first approached me in the chow hall.

"Nephew, I want to give you some paperwork."

"What kind of paperwork?" I asked.

"Well, it's something that can make us strong as black men."

That's when I realized what he was talking about.

"I already am a strong black man," I told him. "And I ain't messing with that gang shit."

"It's not about being in a gang, Tater. It's about *stopping* the violence that gets between us. It's about self-love."

But I knew some of the founding members of the Maryland chapter, and I knew most of what they did was get high and extort people. The original movement might have been about self-love, but these guys had strayed far from the message. I told Bodie I wasn't with it.

"I'm practicing Islam now, Bodie. *There is no God but Allah and Muhammad was his last prophet.* That's all I'm loyal to right now."

Bodie's face got hard. "Nah, you just loyal to Faruq. That's what it is."

Bodie and I didn't speak for several months after that, even though our windows faced one another and we could have easily communicated. I knew he felt like I had betrayed him. He had been watching as I gave more and more of myself to Islam, grew closer to Faruq and farther from him, and now he was forcing the issue. I could follow the code of loyalty I had followed since birth, the code that had me repping 131 building within the projects, Lafayette projects within the city, Baltimore within the prison system. The code that thrives on conflict, that has no end in mind but rivalry. The code that says you can know yourself by knowing who is beneath you. The code that puts you in constant danger, but also promises constant protection. People like my Uncle Bodie lived (and died) by this code, and to be completely honest, it served me well.

Or I could put into practice what meditation taught me—how to rise above. Though it would take years for Bodie to understand this, me not joining the BGF was not about choosing Faruq over Bodie. It simply followed from the realization, the *revelation*, that rivalries never end with one team above the other. All teams, eventually, pull each other down.

22

Looking Ahead

By 1999, my bid was almost up, and it was time to start thinking about my future. My projects were gone. I couldn't go live with my mother, who was practically homeless herself. And I couldn't afford to get a place of my own, given the job prospects out there for convicted felons.

Lil Teddy was the one who convinced me to get married. He and his wife Kim had gotten married in the prison the year before, and he had been a proponent of Kisha ever since he delivered her first letter. I believe he was the one who retrieved the visitors form for me so that I could add her name.

"Boy, you ain't really got no other girl coming to see you like that. Whatchu got to lose?" he said to me one day while we were sitting in the cell.

"Boy, I don't know. I ain't really stressed about Sport Coat." Sport Coat is the dude who messes with your girl while you're locked up. The letter she writes to you, telling you she's leaving you for Sport Coat, that's called a Dear John. I knew I wasn't getting one of those from Kisha. *I'm gonna see you through your bid*, she'd promised during that first visit. And she had.

The wedding took place on May 11th in the visiting room. Teddy was my best man, of course, and his wife Kim was Kisha's matron of honor. YahYah officiated. And we needed one more Muslim witness, so Brother Fred was there, too.

Usually when you get married in jail, they assign a cool officer to the visitors' area so you can get a little time for you and your wife. Kisha and I weren't so lucky. We got the dog lady. The dog lady was this officer who always brought her dog around to do cell searches, and she had it out for me because once I yelled "Get that bitch off my bed!" during a cell search. When she tried to give me an infraction for "disrespecting an officer," I won my case because I was obviously talking about her dog. Anyway, I know she requested to be at my wedding so she could stop me from having quality time with my wife.

That spring, I got a visit from Shang. He seemed like he was doing okay, living up in Essex and working at a swimming pool. He told me stories about the different patrons.

"These African guys, they swim too much! They don't do nothing but go swimming all day every day. That, and mess with the girls in their pool chairs."

"I'd swim all day too, if I could!"

"I don't think they working."

"Whatchu think they doin'?"

"I think they sellin drugs!"

And so on.

Shang started to get me visits from guys I hadn't seen in years. He brought them in twos and threes. First came Cee and Damon Coleman (rest in peace), and then Dietrich and Scooter, Bok and Mookie, and finally Leon and Tank. I didn't realize it at the time, but six of these eight were becoming the Hotboys, a name that would be all over *The Baltimore Sun* in coming years. While I was planning what I'd do when I got out, they were doing everything they could to get themselves in.

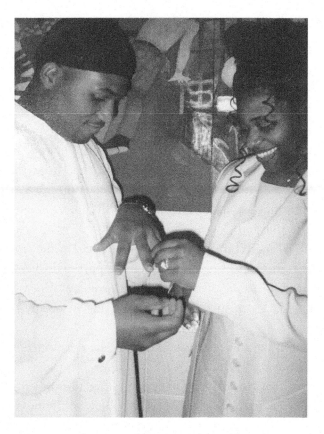

Our wedding (May 11, 1999)

23

The Sundown Prayer

I had four months left in my bid when my father passed away. He died on Pili's birthday. Days later, my mother and all my siblings were together in one room for the first time since I don't know when. The C.O. gave us a private room away from the visiting area, and my mother, Woody, Shang, Quanza, Pili, Kisha and I all piled in.

My mother hugged me for a long time. I had come up with so many mean things to say to her over the past eight years, all along the lines of, *You don't love me, you left me in here.* But when I saw her, I couldn't say any of them. I was just so happy to see her.

"I came to make sure you was alright," she said, once we all sat down. "Are you alright?"

The last conversation I had with my father had taken place a few months earlier, over the phone. He was living in an apartment on Exeter Hall Avenue. We all knew he was sick, but at the time he seemed more stable than I had ever known him. Woody was visiting him that day, so when I called Woody he put the phone to my father's ear.

"What's up, Pops?" I said.

For a moment, all I could hear was coughing.

"In my father's house, there are many mansions," he said at last. "If it were not so, I would have told you." He was reciting from the Gospel of John, the part where Christ assures his disciples that the Father has not abandoned them. I remember thinking that that was ironic.

A few days later, an envelope containing a hundred dollars had arrived in my mail. The return address was listed as Exeter Hall Avenue. I wondered if my father remembered the last time I had taken money from him.

It was strange, feeling the loss of man who had never been a father. Until that hundred dollars came in, he had done nothing for me except show me how not to be. But now a piece of me was gone, and I was surprised to realize that what I felt was grief.

I told my mother I was alright.

And I was, for the most part. At Brockbridge, I was looked up to by the other brothers in the Muslim community, as I had looked up to Faruq. I found out shortly after arriving that Faruq had won his appeal in court and would be getting released, "giving his life sentence back," as we say. I knew the principles of Islam inside and out, and I could speak Arabic well enough to teach it. I got to know Saleem, the imam for the jail, and he made me his assistant imam. We took turns doing the *khutbah* each week.

When it was my turn, I would pick one of the *surahs* to talk about. The one I turned to most often was Surah Al-asr, the contemplation of Salah-asr[5]. It begins:

"By that time, verily, man is at loss. Except those who believe and do righteous deeds, and recommend one another to the truth, and recommend one another to patience."

Verily, man is at loss. That's the part that really hit me when I first read the chapter. It's talking about how, in those late afternoon hours, people begin plotting what they're gonna do when it gets dark. By that time of day, everybody's moving,

---

[5] For you non-Muslim readers, *asr* is one of the five *salah*, or prayer, times. It's the late afternoon prayer. The other four are *fajr* (dawn), *zuhr* (midday), *maghrib* (just after sunset), and *isha* (before midnight).

nobody's mind is on God. It's the time of day when the most car accidents happen. Everyone's thinking, I need to feed the kids, I need to cook dinner, I need to get my hustle on, whatever that may be. The plot begins when nighttime's coming.

I would talk about what nightfall meant in my childhood, when we waited all day for it to get dark. That's when we'd go on our robberies, or pass out testers, or try to sell drugs, or go shoot somebody. It was a real wicked part of the day. It must have been 1500 years ago, too.

On the very last night of 1999, I was glad I was right with my God. Everyone was preparing for the end of the world. Theories flew around the chow hall—either Jesus was coming back, or an earthquake would swallow us all, or the Chesapeake Bay's first ever tsunami was going to wash away the world as we knew it.

At lights out, we were all fully dressed, sitting at the head of our bunks, with the same thought on all our minds—*if these walls start falling in, we getting the fuck out of here.*

I don't remember what time I fell asleep that night. But the next morning, the sun was shining through the window of the dorm. In the hallway, homeboys were greeting each other like they truly hadn't expected to ever meet again in this lifetime.

"Yo we still here, son!"

"We ain't dead!"

"Welcome to the new millennium, motherfuckers!"

Part III

24

The Outside

I was released from prison on June 14, 2000, after six years, two months, and twenty-four days inside. I'll never forget coming out of the gate and seeing Kisha there, in her pink top and black Spandex, waiting for me in the parking lot. All I could think about was how I was going to wear her ass out.

As we came up 295 approaching the city, I saw the new Ravens stadium on the horizon. It was bigger than it looked in the pictures on TV. I had seen Memorial Stadium get replaced by Camden Yards the year I got locked up, but this pretty purple stadium was all that and a bag of chips.

"What's wrong?" Kisha asked. I must've gone silent as I stared out the window.

"Nothing," I said.

"You look like you're upset," she said.

"Naw," I told her. "Just amazed by the view."

Our first stop was to visit my grandparents, who were living in one of the townhomes that replaced the projects' high-rises. After forty years in the projects, from the summer they opened to the summer of their demolition, my grandmother had to move to Westport, in South Baltimore. When they finished building the townhomes, they moved her back. This was my first time seeing Pleasant View Gardens, as they were called. The big circle in the middle of the complex was right where 1101 building used to be.

My grandfather had visited me in jail because Kisha

brought him to see me, but I hadn't seen my grandmother in six years. When we arrived, she was sitting at her table just like always, with something burning on the stove and a Bible in front of her. She was so happy she lived to see me finish that ten no parole.

"Hey baby!" she greeted me as I walked in the door. "It's good to see you home."

She wasn't ever one for tears and drama. I was only most recent in a long line of sons and nephews and grandsons she had seen come home from prison.

"Thanks, Granny," I said.

She went to the stove and prepared a plate for me. I had that plate clean in about three minutes flat. In the chow hall, your group has to stand up as soon as the group behind yours sits down, so eating fast is one of the hardest prison habits to break. The only thing slowing me down was the fork and knife, actually, 'cause I'd gotten used to eating everything with a spoon. My own brother Shang was the reason for that; after he stabbed someone in the head with a fork in Hagerstown, knives and forks were removed from all the prisons.

Granny and I talked for a while at the table. She told me how much she liked "my little friend Dietrich," who visited her often while I was in prison and gave her money to send me. When I finally got up to leave, she grabbed my hand.

"You gonna stay out here now?" she asked.

I promised her I would.

As Kisha pulled out of the circle where the old Lafayette rec center still stood, I saw a slim dude with an Adidas t-shirt on running across the street. It was Shang.

"What's up Fat Tater!" he called, grinning from ear to ear. I jumped out of the car and gave him a big hug. It had been a few months since I'd seen him.

"Get in," I told him. "Let's go see Moms."

He hopped in the backseat and Kisha drove us up Douglass projects, where my mother was living with one of her friends. She was real happy to see me and I was happy to see her. I could tell she and her friend and her friend's husband had been getting high before we got there. Looking around the apartment, I was glad I married Kisha and didn't need somewhere to stay.

The next stop on our reunion tour was Kisha's mom's house. She lived in Randallstown off Liberty Road with Kisha's grandmother and one of her older brothers. Remembering how they used to hang up on me when I called, I didn't expect a warm welcome and I didn't get one. They looked at me like I was the downfall of their daughter and sister. Kisha had, after all, married a convicted felon who had come home to not a pot to piss in or a window to throw it out of.

While we were at Kisha's mom's place, I got a call from Leon on Kisha's cell phone. He told me he was about to go to Disney World and that his flight was leaving in a couple of hours.

"Meet me at Mondawmin Mall," he told me. "I wanna give you something."

So Kisha and I left her family and she dropped me off at Mondawmin. As soon as I got out the car, I spotted Leon coming out USA Boutique with my boys Tank and Donnell Booker, a bag of Bally shoes and flowered silk shirts hanging off each arm. They waved me over.

"What's up Fat Tater! You ain't even fat no more!" Leon pulled me into a hug.

It was a quick meeting, because Leon had to make his flight, but before they left, Leon and Tank each handed me a stack of money.

I counted the stacks only after I got home. They had given me about two and half thousand dollars in total. My first thought was, *Why did I just take the subway home?* With all that cash in my pocket, I could've easily paid for a hack. My second thought was, *How much are Leon and them making right now?*

25

The Hotboys

As it turned out, my little homeboys were running the streets and making a *lot* of money. My second day home, I had to check in with my parole officer on Guilford Avenue. I didn't have a way to get there, so I asked Bok to come get me. He told me he was busy, but gave me the keys to his brand new 1999 LS 400 Lexus and a cell phone, and told me to call him when I was finished. When I pulled up to the parole place on Guilford Avenue, a couple of dudes I was bidding with were standing outside. Their jaws just about dropped when they saw me.

"You looking good in that new whip!" my man Black Man called out.

"Man, this Bok shit," I explained. "I needed a way to get here and he just handed me the keys to this motherfucker."

I wound up giving Black Man a ride down Jefferson Street, because I was living in the 2200 block of Jefferson and that's where he was going.

The next day, I had more business to tend to, and I needed another ride. So Leon handed me the keys to his 1999 GS Lexus. He told me he had dropped thirty-seven thousand dollars on that car in three weeks.

"Boy, you getting it!" I said as I took the keys.

"Fat Tater, we the Hotboys!" he said, and we laughed.

The next day, they called me and asked if I wanted to go to Six Flags. We all met up at Church Square down Deakyland and piled into about thirty cars, all luxury vehicles. Lexus GS's,

LS's, the '99 Yukon, and maybe five of them Lexus Coupes. On the way, we had to pull the whole caravan over on 695 because none of us knew how to get anywhere. It was a lot of arguing over who could and could not drive.

When we got there, Bok, Leon and Scooter paid everyone's way. It reminded me of our gas station days, except this time the bill was about four thousand dollars, and they paid it like it was nothing. Except Scooter, of course; he did everything to wiggle out of paying.

Before entering the water park, we stopped to shoot for teddy bears at one of those game booths. I knew none of my homeboys really cared about hitting the shot or getting a teddy bear. They just wanted to stunt. Bok paid for like twenty shots, and pretty soon the hoop game became a gambling spot. Dudes were on the side making bets and mad people were gathering to watch. It was clear these guys had at least fifty grand on them altogether. One shot was like a two or three thousand dollar pot, and they had all the money on the ground in the middle of an amusement park. They turned Six Flags into a Vegas casino. These were the Hotboys for real.

That weekend, it was a party up in the Teamsters Union Hall on Erdman Avenue. I walked in and saw dudes from everywhere—up the hill, down the hill, the projects, Harford Road, Belair Road, over West, you name it. I got so drunk I took a piss in the middle of the dance floor.

At some point, I started talking to my homeboy Dre and his brother Yae Yae, cousins of Muggsy Bogues who grew up in 131 building with me. Dre was explaining to me that he didn't like Bok for some bullshit reason. He also mentioned that he had his clique with him from the Boulevard. Next thing I knew, one of those dudes was slashing Bok across the face with a broken Hennessey bottle, and then all hell broke loose and somebody was lying dead on the ground.

I was caught off guard. I was still living in the old world, before I went to jail, when the Lafayette boys rarely had conflict with anyone. I made my way to the door as fast as I could.

Outside, I jumped in with my homeboy Pooh Pooh, who was driving Leon's big green Chevy Suburban over the medium strip because traffic was backed up along the road. Leon was cursing Pooh Pooh out from the passenger seat—*you stupid motherfucker, you making us hot the way you driving!* I was fed up with all the drama. I told them niggas to take me home.

It wasn't long before I found out that some of my homies were being charged with the murder and people were saying I was involved. This was the post-demolition world I talked about, the one that arose from the ashes of the projects. Dudes had to fight over territory now, kill each other over words. It felt like anyone could get caught up in any moment.

But I hadn't done enough partying yet. Keep in mind, I was twenty-six years old and had spent all my twenties thus far in a jail cell. I still caught myself wearing shoes in the shower sometimes. So when Leon showed up at my door at 11 p.m. on the Fourth of July asking if I was trying to go out, I said yes right away.

"Cool, we going to a white party in Towson," he said.

"But I don't have no fresh white shit to wear!"

"You're good man, Da Da's is open!"

"Da Da's? Where's that?"

"Monument Street. Let's go."

I couldn't believe there was a clothing store open this close to midnight. But Mike, the owner, made millions off the community by keeping those hours. Leon and I got ourselves some all-white gear, jumped back in his GS Lexus Bubble Eye, and hit 83 going north. I asked him where everybody was at and he told me they were waiting for us.

The party was in a ballroom at the Sheraton Inn in Towson. To my prison-trained eyes, the hotel looked like a palace. When we got inside, it was the whole Hotboys clique—Leon, Bok, Tiger, Manny El, Scooter, Keithy, Mookie, Dooky Butt Gary, Tank, Crutty Mone, Lil Stink, DJ, everybody for real. The party was definitely popping. I went over to the bar to see what my boys were up to. No good, as usual. Scooter had the bartender chick locked down. He kept throwing money behind the bar and stealing fifths of liquor while she and the other bartenders bent down to pick up the money. We got drunk off his scamming.

At some point, I got to talking with Bok. He told me he was proud of the man he had become.

"I take good care of all my boys now, Tater," he told me. It was true. He had purchased a luxury car for each of his little homies. He walked around with fifty thousand dollars in his bookbag and a gun in his waistband. Later, when I visited his apartment on Perring Parkway, he showed me his box of money. There was half a million dollars in there, he said. It was so heavy that the bottom started to break when he tried to lift it.

When I looked up, all the Hotboys were throwing money in the club. They probably threw about twenty grand altogether. Even I was grabbing money off the floor by the end.

26

The Seafood Salad

Nine days after I got home, Woody and I had gone down to the temp agency on the top floor of the Pratt Street Power Plant. I applied for and got a job with Northern Pipeline Construction. Woody went through the whole process with me, got himself a job, even went and took the piss test. But when Monday rolled around, Woody told me he was staying home. "I ain't want the job," he told me. "I just wanted you to go get a job."

It's funny. Putting this all into writing makes me realize for the first time how much Woody has given me in the way of redirection. I always thought it was Shang who was generous, with his cash and his Adidas, while Woody kept everything he got for himself. Now I see they both were trying to set me up for greatness in their own way.

My job at Northern Pipeline Construction kept me busy Monday through Friday, so I couldn't go to jummah on Friday mornings anymore. Instead, I went on Sundays with Kisha and India to the New Psalmist Baptist Church out on Patterson Avenue. It was our family time. India and I would watch Kisha sing in the choir, and sometimes one of our friends would speak from the pulpit. Don't get me wrong, I didn't want to be no Christian. My belief in Islam was as strong as ever. But Islam says to respect Jesus as a messenger of God, even if we don't believe he was God himself. I believe in the testaments, I believe in the miracle birth, and all that, because Islam says to believe in it. I never felt like I was committing *shirk*. It's all in the Qu'ran.

Still, my church attendance got me in trouble with my Muslim brothers. Once I got caught up in a revival at New Psalmist, not realizing there was a camera crew present. The cameras caught me clapping and cheering and praising like I'd just witnessed a miracle with my own two eyes. And apparently my homeboy Travis saw me on television in the dayroom back at Jessup, and he told all my Muslim brothers. I guess the news spread quickly. I had been assistant imam, remember. I had taught half those brothers Arabic! I still get shit for that revival footage. Not too long ago, I ran into my old cell buddy Lil Teddy, and he said, "You know the last time I saw you? On Dr. Walker Scott Thomas' television channel, praising the Lord!"

Working a steady job also meant that I saw less of the Hotboys as the year went on. By the spring of the following year, I was only hanging with those guys on the weekends, and only because they paid my way. Every Friday and Saturday night, they were leaving twenty grand on the floor of some club.

In early May, I heard through the grapevine that some kid from North Avenue had stolen money from them, and that Bok had beat him up. Then I heard it went to the guns. Then the North Avenue boys kidnapped Bok's wife Buffy and tried to kill her. She survived, but the revenge shootings started going back and forth. By the time Memorial Day rolled around, the Lafayette Hotboys and the North Avenue boys were outright hunting each other.

That night, Dietrich came and got me to take me to a block party. On the way, we stopped at Dietrich's girl's house at the intersection of Sinclair and Moravia. Her family was having a potluck. Her mother opened the door and told us we could eat anything but the seafood salad, 'cause that was being saved for her husband. Greedy ol' me, I ate the seafood salad along with everything else. By the time her husband got there, I had polished off the whole thing. The lady fussed me out some kind of terrible.

But that seafood salad saved my life. Because meanwhile, at the block party, the Hotboys had allegedly shown up and a major shooting had gone down. Eleven people were shot, and a girl was dead.[6] Rumor had it she was the girlfriend of one of the North Avenue boys.

I knew the investigators would come for me, because all my friends had allegedly been at the scene of the shooting. Shit, I *would* have been there if Dietrich hadn't wanted to see his girl. But when asked about my whereabouts during the shooting, I could say truthfully that I was at the house on Sinclair and Moravia. And the lady could testify to me being there, because she remembered fussing me out about the seafood salad. She told the investigators that we would have had to have turned into demons and gotten to North Avenue at the speed of light, because she saw news of the shooting on television just five minutes after we left.

After the Memorial Day shooting, as it became known in the papers, all the Hotboys came under federal investigation for drug conspiracy. I saw their pictures on the news, along with the fact that the Feds were looking for them. Mind you, I had nothing to do with their business endeavors. They were careful not to tell me anything, and I never asked. But I had rented a few cars for them under my name and was in regular contact with them, so every day I went to work paranoid. Sure enough, the police showed up at my job one day while I was fixing a gas leak behind Mayor O'Malley's house on Walther Boulevard.

They took me down to the ATF headquarters on Remington and 28th and told me I was being held for conspiracy to distribute cocaine and heroin, as well as a couple of murder investigations. The cop who questioned me was

---

[6] Her name was Lakeisha Monich Moten, and she was 24 years old.

Sergeant Kim, the first hard Korean cop I'd ever met. I said nothing the whole time, except to ask for some food because I had just dug a deep ass hole. Finally, Kim told me to give them a call if I heard from Bok, and let me go.

Then they followed me for weeks. To work, to church, to pick India up from school, you name it. One Wednesday, while Kisha and I were at Bible study at New Psalmist, a woman slid up next to Kisha and whispered, "He knows where Bok is."

To this day, Kisha swears that woman was sent from God to warn her that I was putting the Hotboys before our family. At the time of the Memorial Day shooting, she was about eight months pregnant.

"That lady didn't know me from Adam!" she'll say to me.

"Kisha, she was the police..." I'll say back.

Those were the kinds of tricks they pulled.

The Feds also harassed Kisha while I was at work. They would show up at the house, threatening to take India away, even the unborn baby, if Kisha didn't cooperate with them. They used her pregnancy against her, tried to scare her into speech. Luckily, she knew even less than the nothing I knew.

Against the darkness of that summer, two bright moments stand out in my memory. The first was the birth of my and Kisha's daughter, Mook-Mook, on June 30, 2001. On the television in the corner of the hospital room, Shaq was leading the Lakers to victory in the NBA finals. The delivery doctor and I watched as Kisha labored between us. "I'm in all this pain," she kept saying, "and here y'all are talking about the Lakers!"

The second was my homeboy Day Day's wedding. When Day Day and his fiancé Ebony visited me during my bid, Day Day told me he was waiting for me to get out so I could be the best man at his wedding. So on July 7, 2001, I stood beside him in a cathedral in Philly as he and Ebony became husband and wife.

Back in Baltimore, the Feds found Bok and everybody else they wanted to find. But they weren't finished with me. For a second time, I was picked up, brought downtown, and interrogated. This time, the interrogation was led by a little old lady named Marcia Wade from the D.E.A.

"I don't have time for games, Mr. Barksdale," she warned me. "I have questions."

She listed off a bunch of names, including Anthony Jones, and I told her I knew all of them. Most were childhood friends, in fact.

"I'm not playing with you," she said again. "I've put a lot of violent offenders away. And let me tell you, I'm sick and tired of hearing about all this violence."

Must be rough, I thought. *Hearing* about all this violence.

While they were interrogating me, I could hear Kisha and my brother Woody praying loudly outside the room. *Release Him in the name of Jesus! Release Him in the name of Jesus!* They were practically shouting. The Feds could hear them, too.

In the end, they told me there was going to be a new federal indictment and that I may or may not be part of it. That was on a Tuesday. I went home and bit my fingers for three days. On Friday, they released the indictment on Fox News. I was glued to the television all morning. When the twelve names and pictures appeared on the screen, and mine was not among them, it felt like being released from prison all over again.

Eleven of the Hotboys copped out to lesser charges. Bok got thirty-five years, Leon got thirty, Crutty Mone got fifteen, Dietrich got ten, and everyone else got something in between. After Memorial Day, there had been talk of the death penalty, so in my eyes they were lucky. But the luckiest was the twelfth Hotboy, my man Elijah. He went to trial and was acquitted.

At twenty-three, Crutty Mone was the oldest of the Hotboys. I heard there was a lot of chaos in the bullpen during the trials because it was a room full of teenagers and twenty-somethings who knew each other like family. They were in there wrestling, rapping, calling each other names, all kinds of nonsense. The police even gave them M&M's to incentivize good behavior, and they just threw them at each other.

During the sentencing, the judge asked Bok if he understood that pleading guilty meant he would get 35 years and all his boys would get less. When Bok agreed, Judge Motts gave him an approving look. "Then you guys are smarter than I thought you were," he said.

27

Crispy King

After that whole mess, I lost my job at Northern Pipeline. For the next few years, I bounced back and forth between the streets and various jobs. I tried selling weed and doing the rap music thing with Cee for a while. It paid the bills; we sold about a hundred pounds of weed per week on Belnord and Orleans Street. When that well dried up, I got a job unloading trains on the waterfront. That was fine for a while, but then I had an altercation with my supervisor and wound up back on the streets. Which was fine with me, too, because the job hadn't paid me enough to quit hustling, anyway.

In that period, I spent a lot of time on the phone with Bodie, who was locked up in the Supermax. He had gotten booked again after being found with a gun under the seat of his car.

"This lawyer's gonna get me off, though," he assured me. "He told me I have nothing to worry about."

Bodie's lawyer was an Italian guy who had watched every season of *The Wire* and loved the Avon Barksdale character. His entire argument was that no one checks under their seat before they sit down in a car. The car had belonged to one of Bodie's friends, not to Bodie—*and who*, the lawyer asked, *looks below the seat before sitting down in a friend's car?*

During the trial, the lawyer got up and taped a water gun to the bottom of the prosecutor's chair while the court was in recess. Then, just before closing arguments began, he began passing Life Savers out to the jurors and whispering, "Save Avon Barksdale's life!"

The judge saw him. "If you don't have enough Life Savers for everyone," he said, "don't give them to anyone."

When it came time for the defense's closing argument, Bodie's lawyer walked over to the prosecutor's chair. He bent down, untaped the water gun, and held it up, addressing the jury. "Like I said, no one looks under their seat before sitting down." He sprayed some water in their direction and they all laughed. The jury left and came back within minutes. "Not guilty" on all charges.

After quitting my job on the waterfront, I opened up a dope shop in front of the Crispy King on Fayette between Caroline and Central, a block from where the projects once stood. My connect told me he had a "missile on the blow," meaning some real good heroin. He bought me about $25,000 worth and we split it evenly. I made enough to pay him back within three days, and after that I was clearing about ten thousand a day. This kid Tony had been selling ready rock on the corner before I got there, but after three weeks of me selling all that blow in his face, he finally joined me. I organized two different crews from up Chapel Hill. Those dudes had been groomed well. They never messed my money up and everything was straight.

Still, that old feeling of restlessness came over me, same as I felt at Hagerstown. Even in high school, hustling on its own had never felt productive enough. I realized I wasn't happy unless I was learning something new, whether that was football or Arabic or plain old reading and writing. The college program on The Farm hadn't worked out, but now I finally had the time and money to get a real college degree. I could practically feel Woody pushing me across the street to Sojourner-Douglass College, where he had gone. I decided to apply and I got in. Even better, the school faced the Crispy King, so I could keep an eye on my dope shop while I was in class. Whenever I saw the police Big Country in the covert position, I could warn my lookout. It was the most convenient thing in the world.

One morning early in the summer of 2007, I pulled up in front of Crispy King with my boy Chim to check on my shop. I was driving a 1999 Chevy Tahoe and we were smoking half a vick of Purple Haze. One of my runners came up to my window and gave me some bread; business was good. While I was idling there, my homie Freaky came up and asked us for a ride up Deakyland. I asked if he was dirty.

"Because I'm already putting this loud in me, and I don't want to get pulled over for anything else," I said.

"Nah, just let me hop in," he said, so I did.

As we approached Clay Courts in Deakyland, I saw a narc car in the alley. I made a sharp turn, but they came around the corner and met me at the intersection of Chase and Bond. The officers pulled out their guns and yanked all three of us out of the car. One of them was Daniel Hersl, infamous at that time for making arrests based on nothing and taking bribes for release. When they patted us down, they found drugs in the crotch of Freaky's pants. Hersl got excited and pointed at me. "Take his ass too!" he yelled. "He has too much fucking mouth. Lock his ass up and charge him with conspiracy."

Hersl took thirty-five hundred dollars from me, and I spent four days in jail because I arrived on a Friday. The charges were eventually dropped, but I never got back that money or time.

28

The Orange T-Shirts

Towards the end of the summer I ran into my old friend and Muslim brother Hamza at the laundromat in Erdman Shopping Center. I had just slammed the dryer door closed when I heard a "Hey Tater, what's up?" behind me, and there he was. I hadn't seen Hamza since I left Patuxent.

"What's up Hamza! What's happening boy, you just got home?"

"Yeah I *just* got home," he said.

"How much time you do altogether?"

"Twenty-two years."

"Damn, son."

We talked for a while, reminiscing, shaking our heads. I asked what he was up to now.

"Nothing, man, you know, I just be doing side jobs. I got attempted murders and all kinds of crazy stuff on my record, so you know ain't nobody gon' give me no job."

He jerked his thumb to the parking lot. "I'm hauling trash right now. I got a truck, so shoot, I'm just going around hauling trash for stores, you know. I'm a licensed plumber. I'm doing what I need to do, I'ma be good."

"That's good, man, it's good to hear that." I turned to check the time left on my clothes.

"But you know, Faruq just started this program," he began, and I turned back to him.

"What kind of program?"

"We doing this lil outreach thing, you know, we trying to get dudes to stop the killings."

I laughed. It was a *yeah, okay* laugh, and Hamza heard it.

"Where the fuck you gon' do that at?"

"We out in McElderry Park right now, just in the neighborhood."

"Over Jefferson Street, Monument, all that?"

"Yeah, that whole area."

"Boys rough as shit down there! They down there killing the shit out each other!"

"Yeah man, that's why we trying to get on it! It's one of the most dangerous neighborhoods in America! The health department started this program, and Faruq gon' facilitate it, and we gon' work, you know, we gon' try to stop the killings."

"Well, I wish you all the luck in the world, brother," I said.

"You should stop past!" he said. "I know Faruq wants to see you."

I figured he might. The last time I had seen Faruq was the week I came home from prison. I came home on a Wednesday, and that Friday I went to jummah at Masjid Al-Haqq behind the Shake and Bake on Pennsylvania Avenue. Faruq was there, and after the service he offered me a ride home.

I had spent the past two days, remember, partying with my homeboys. They had collectively given me about twenty thousand dollars, and I had been able to give Kisha about half a year's rent in those first two days. My homeboys' lifestyle was looking good to my broke ass. So when Faruq offered to drive me home that day, I decided I didn't want him to know where I stayed. I knew he'd be on me, checking in all the time, and I didn't want that. He was on some positive shit, and I just wanted to get paid. So I asked him to drop me off at my grandmother's house in Pleasant View Gardens.

As I was getting out the car in front of my grandmother's, Faruq handed me two folded twenty-dollar bills. I didn't act bougie, I didn't say nothing about my homeboys, I just took it and thanked him and left. I had avoided him ever since.

Soon after my run-in with Hamza at the laundromat, I spotted him and Faruq in my rearview mirror as I drove down Monument. I ducked low in my seat and looked back only once I was a good distance away. They were easy to pick out in their bright orange T-shirts, talking intently to a group of dudes on the corner of Monument and Belnord. What they were doing, I would learn later, was called *canvassing*—asking around the neighborhood to find out who had done what, and who was mad enough to shoot somebody over it. All I could see in that moment, though, were Hamza and Faruq's giant ID badges pinned to their sweat-drenched T-shirts. Safe Streets didn't have an office yet, so the outreach workers stayed outside all day, on full display to anybody driving past. No part of it appealed to me.

But over the next few months, I kept hearing about this Safe Streets program from different sources. And then one day, Kisha came home and handed me a piece of paper with Faruq's name and number written on it. She had just come from picking the girls up from school, and she had overheard some parents talking about a dude named Leon Faruq giving out jobs to former felons and violent offenders. Naturally, Kisha had butted into the conversation on my behalf.

"Oh yeah? My husband need a job," she said. "His ass need to get off the street. Who he need to contact?"

A dude named Gerrod wrote down Faruq's name and number and gave it to her. As soon as she saw the name, Kisha started laughing. "Oh, my husband know him! They was locked up together. I remember Faruq from the visiting room."

With that piece in paper in hand, I thought about what having steady legal work would mean. Ever since beating Hersl's phony charges, I'd been feeling tired in a way that had nothing to do with sleep. I was tired of getting locked up, of getting robbed by police, of having to keep an eye out at all times. I just wanted to be able to go to work, come home, and chill the fuck out. I wanted a regular job. And it seemed the universe had one in mind for me.

Faruq told me I had to volunteer before I could get hired. And before I could volunteer, I had to be interviewed by all the current outreach workers.

When I arrived at the new office on Port and Monument, there were about eight dudes sitting around a table. The only two I recognized were Hamza and Faruq. This immediately threw me off; six out of eight was a high ratio of strangers for me to be dealing with in East Baltimore. One of them turned out to be my homeboy Biggie from jail, who I hadn't recognized because he wasn't big anymore and he went by Jermaine. I sat down and the guys started grilling me. Who was I? Who was I affiliated with? Who had respect for me?

Well, I got mad. I banged my fist on the table.

"Check this out, b," I said. "I don't know none of y'all. But my name is Fat Tater, I'm from Lafayette projects, and I'm g'ed up. I grew up with all those lil dudes out there shooting each other. I know them Chapel Hill boys. I know the lil Meats, I know the Fat Rellys, I know all them."

What value could I bring to this program?

"I'm telling you, I *know* these dudes," I said again. "They respect me. If you don't believe me, let's walk down Monument Street together."

So we did. By the time we got to Milton Avenue, at least five dudes had said what's up to me, and I had been offered a position with Safe Streets.

29

Safe Streets

Safe Streets Baltimore launched in 2007, and was based on the Cure Violence model developed at the University of Illinois School of Public Health in 1995. Safe Streets was actually the first implementation of Cure Violence outside of Chicago. The idea behind Cure Violence is that prevention reduces violence more effectively than prosecution. And the people most qualified to prevent violence in a particular neighborhood are the people who live there—people who have themselves been both perpetrators and victims of violence. As veterans of street life, these outreach workers know what type of situations are likely to end in a shooting, and what might be said to stop one from happening. There is no stopping and frisking, no seizure of drugs or guns, no beating the fight out of people. There are conversations and follow-ups and relationships built; community policing, in other words, as policing should be.

As of the writing of this book, Cure Violence has programs in Baltimore, New York, Philadelphia, New Orleans, Kansas City, and a host of other cities in the United States and abroad. Baltimore, as I mentioned, was the first after Chicago, so the original Safe Streets team was trained by the CeaseFire guys (as the Chicago program was known back then).

The weekend after I was brought on as a volunteer, there was a symposium on gun violence held at the Douglass Myers Museum—the same building where Crutty Mone and Michael and I found bricks to build a raft more than two decades earlier. When I arrived, I saw that half the chairs were filled with Safe Streets dudes and the other half with teenagers on probation who were required to be there. A microphone was being passed around. The Safe Streets dudes were discussing program's mission. The kids weren't having it.

"Shit, man, if I feel like shooting somebody, ain't nobody coming to tell me what I'm gon' do!" one of them called out.

"Yeah, well, in our neighborhood, people got respect for us, so that's how it work," one of the outreach workers called back. "If we was in your neighborhood, we would have your big homeboys, you know, the ones who killed people, that's who would be telling you not to shoot nobody." He was trying to explain one of the fundamentals of Safe Streets: that communities can police themselves better than anyone else can. But none of the outreach workers were all that polished yet, since we'd all just started working, so it quickly became a kind of shouting match.

They went back and forth until Faruq approached the podium to make his speech. This was the first time I had ever seen him visibly upset. Angry, even. He talked about how frustrated he was with the conditions of Baltimore—he was from D.C., remember—and with the dialogue he was hearing. I realized then that he was actually serious about stopping gun violence. I mean, I knew whatever Faruq chose to do, he was really about it, but I had wondered if he really believed it was possible. As imam, he had refused to go with the prison flow. If someone did something that would get him stabbed anywhere else, Faruq would step in and make sure that didn't happen. It seemed he intended to use the same methods to decrease conflict in the community as he had used to decrease conflict in prison. And I couldn't argue with his methods; they had worked on me, after all.

In February of 2008, after volunteering for three months, I was hired full-time and assigned to the McElderry Park site. Since Safe Streets had been implemented in McElderry Park, the community had gone 23 months without a homicide. But there had been plenty of non-fatal shootings, and sometimes only a few lucky inches separated the two.

My first day at work, I participated in what we called a briefing. These were held in the office every night before the shift began, and they gave us a chance to talk about potential conflicts brewing in the community: who was coming home from prison, who had been used as a prosecution witness, who they told on, who was new and trying to hustle on corners already occupied, and so on. A couple guys mentioned that they wanted to follow up with mediations they had done the day before, to make sure nobody had changed their minds overnight. Keep the conflict "cool," as they said. During that first briefing, I wanted to show that I would be useful. So I offered to serve as a buffer for the Bloods on Belnord Avenue, because I knew Cee's nephew hung with those dudes, and he and I had a good rapport. (His name was also Cee, but you can't have a name with a *C* in it when you hang with Bloods, so he went by T.E., for Tough Enough.) After the briefing, we went out to canvass the neighborhood. The sky was already dark.

One of our strategies was just to go to each corner and ask the kids standing around if they were planning to kill someone that night. My first shift, I surprised a lot of people with that question. "Tater, what the fuck you doing?" was a common response.

"I'm with Safe Streets now!" I would tell them. "We out here to stop the killing!"

Most dudes laughed at that, the same way I had laughed at Hamza in the laundromat.

"This motherfucker..." they would say. "That shit is a cover-up for some drug ring or something, why the fuck they hire you?"

Hamza told me later that he even received some phone calls from dudes asking why he hired one of the biggest dope dealers in East Baltimore. They weren't wrong to ask; I was in the streets just weeks before. It was only when I knew I'd have a steady paycheck that I finally got rid of the last of my dope.

But Hamza knew what I knew, what I had tried to get across in my interview—that my reputation as a hustler would help the Safe Streets mission, more than any amount of training could. No one would suspect alliance with BPD. Nobody could accuse me of not understanding.

That question, though, *Are you gonna kill someone today*, made the kids uncomfortable, and I understood completely. It had only been a few months since I had ducked at the sight of those orange T-shirts, rolled my eyes at the idea of "violence interruption." It had been even less time since I myself was out on the corner, planning the night's mischief as the sun went down. And while I had never been a shooter, I can't claim that was a moral decision—people were just too afraid of my last name to pick fights with me, and if they did, I had other people to do the shooting for me.

When we were little and hustling in the projects, we all had guns, all different kinds—nine millimeters, pistol grips, you name it. We never planned on shooting anybody, but we didn't want anyone to think we *couldn't*. It was large amounts of money and dope being passed around. We needed something to scare off the stick-up boys and the police. Whenever Melvin Russell pulled up in front of the building, someone would shoot a few bullets into the ground, just to slow him up. In the second that he paused getting out of the car, we'd run up into somebody's apartment. Safe.

I never needed to shoot anyone in the projects because we were family. When we fought, we fought with our hands. But even after the projects were gone, and I was hustling outside the Crispy King, I never had plans to shoot nobody. For one thing, I never really ran into no problems. People knew I could fight, and more importantly, they knew I could call on Bodie. Or Shang, or Cee, or Leon, or Mone, or any of the Hotboys before they got locked up. And just so people didn't forget what I *could* do, I would come around and flash, pulling my gun out from my waistband like "Y'all like this one?" Show them something that would stick in their minds. Then I would put the gun away, and be normal.

So it didn't feel hypocritical to canvass with Safe Streets. We weren't telling dudes to stop selling drugs or stop getting high or stop making money. We were just asking them not to kill anybody over drugs and money. And, like I said, I had never been a shooter.

Eventually, in response to the kids' discomfort, I would learn to say, "How you're feeling right now, you should be *that* uncomfortable when you're about to shoot someone over something petty."

We walked around McElderry Park for what felt like an eternity that first night. It was around one in the morning when I started asking myself what the fuck I got myself into. I knew the shift went through two a.m. for good reason; I knew exactly the kind of shit that went on in those wee hours. But this was the first time in years that I had to be somewhere for eight hours straight. Even though nothing much happened that first night, I was exhausted by the time I climbed into my Chevy Tahoe at the end of my shift.

30

The Numbers

I saw my first shooting response my second night on the job. It was a small one, because no one really knew the dude who had been killed. Some Safe Streets guys had passed out flyers, knocked on doors, tried to let people know we were about to do a vigil, but it's hard to get people to mourn more than they already have to. It ended up being maybe ten of us interrupters and a group of Christian Reformed brothers. They stood in a circle and prayed, while Faruq and Hamza and I stood off to the side. The whole thing lasted about twenty-five minutes.

Depending on the outcome of the shooting, a shooting response looks like a vigil, or a march, or a prayer, or a speak-out. Usually, we ask the victim's family and friends what they want us to do. Sometimes people want to keep quiet about it, so we just pass out flyers reminding people that violence at this pace isn't normal.

I saw my second shooting response a few weeks later. This time, we had to do crowd control. It was a speak-out, and Faruq was on the bullhorn, stirring up the crowd.

"What do we want?"

"SAFE STREETS!"

"When do we want them?"

"NOW!"

Then Faruq started citing statistics. Thirty three thousand—that's how many people get gunned down in the street every year in this country. When I heard that number, I wasn't ready for it. I knew it was a lot of dudes getting killed, but thirty three thousand, that's worse than war. That's a hundred thousand dudes every three years.

Three hundred fifty—that's how many murders in Baltimore per year. This was a number I had heard before, but I had also heard Chicago had six hundred, so I thought we were at least doing better than them. Then Faruq explained how you have to count murders per capita. Considering Baltimore's population of 620,000 against Chicago's population of 2.8 million, Baltimore doesn't look better anymore. It looks about four times worse.

That was the day shit started getting real to me. Like, damn. We really bought into this street shit. The powers that be, the rich motherfuckers, the policy makers, they set this shit in motion. They don't just want us dead. They want us to kill each other.

31

Strategies

There is a motto for survival you hear a lot around here: "In the streets, it's better to be feared than loved." Growing up, I heard this all the time. It means disrespect has to be met with violence, or else you're soft, and soft dudes don't last.

I'd be lying if I said I changed overnight. About three weeks after I was hired, I saw Cee and T.E. on Belnord Avenue. I pulled up alongside them and rolled down the window.

"Cee, boy you better get with this Safe Streets shit!" I called out. "I just got my first check. They paying us just to hang out around here and tell dudes not to kill each other!" By that point, every corner in the area had been assigned to someone Cee or I knew. It was almost like old times.

"Ain't nobody with that rat-ass snitching-ass shit!" T.E. yelled back, looking straight into my face.

"Whatchu say?" I asked, opening my car door.

The irony of the fistfight that followed—the fact that I was using violence to promote Safe Streets—didn't even occur to me.

Some Safe Streets dudes still operate this way, to be honest. Some could potentially be shooters. We just pray they *don't* shoot, because we need that type of person around to squash beefs.

Most of the time, it's straight bullshit that gets people killed. A guy disrespects a guy some kind of way, looks at him wrong, looks at his girl wrong, bumps into him, borrows some money and doesn't pay it back. There's so much to beef about. It's never nothing major, nobody is ever taking a hundred thousand dollars. It's fifty dollars, or maybe three hundred. But little things get bigger when he's BGF and he's not, when everybody involved got cousins and friends.

When I mediate, I make sure both guys know I'm on their side. "Man, you know he a punk, why you gon' shoot him?" I appeal to their reason. "That man don't want no trouble, and you don't want no trouble neither, 'cause you getting money. I just need both of y'all to let that shit go." It's no different, really, from what I used to do on the street. Dudes work as part-time mediators on every street corner in America, trying to cool each other down before the police show up and nobody makes any money that day.

Sometimes I make a point of telling dudes how lucky they are, that so-and-so was going to shoot them if not for our interference, so they'd better stay their ass away. Sometimes the aggressor himself will ask for our help in keeping dudes away, so that they don't have to shoot nobody.

There's usually a fix. Take a situation where one dude is using the same color tops as someone else with a good product, knowing that his product isn't as good. Of course that's gonna piss the other dude off, but there's a resolution to this problem where nobody gets killed—the second dude changes color before it goes to the guns.

Other dudes have different tactics. Like I said, we need the rough-around-the-edges type around to squash some beefs. They're the type people see and think, *This motherfucker mean what the fuck he say.* The type to make you forget he's wearing a bright orange T-shirt.

They'll put their hands on a dude and say, "What the fuck you doing! You over there shooting, my nephew was around there!" Even if their nephew wasn't anywhere near there— making it personal works to their advantage.

It's not always dudes fighting over bruised egos, though. Violence can erupt out of just about anybody. About a month after I was hired, I was standing on the corner of Monument Street and Montford Avenue with Hamza, when we saw a flood of little girls coming towards each other from either end of Montford, getting ready to fight. As we watched, the mother of some of the girls pulled up in her car and started distributing baseball bats. Hamza and I were at her car window in about thirty seconds. We explained that her children would be charged with attempted murder, or even murder, if someone got hurt in this rumble.

"And look," I said, pointing up at the camera attached to the side of the building behind us. "You gon' send your kids to jail! The police gon' have your tags *and* footage of you handing out these bats."

That made her come to her senses. With her help, and the help of older brothers who came running to the scene, we got everyone to put their bats down.

32

Public Relations

While I was learning how to keep things calm in McElderry Park, Faruq was teaching me to agitate the public. He knew who I was in prison. He knew that I was loud and that I liked giving speeches; he had heard that I did the khutbahs at Brockbridge. After that second shooting response, he told me the rest were all mine. I got on that bullhorn the first chance I got and went off. I talked about dudes giving dudes bad drugs and expecting to be paid. I talked about dudes killing dudes for petty issues. I talked about mental health, financial stability, you name it. I could see Faruq was proud.

So it felt like a test when, a year after I was hired, he asked me to walk through McElderry Park with two white guys and a video camera. I looked at him sideways—he and I both knew how that would affect my image—but I trusted his instincts.

I led the reporters down Monument Street. As we passed the clothing store Prophets, I saw this dude Black Rome watching us from the doorway. He started snickering like a little kid.

"What we need is resources," I said loudly to the reporters, making sure he could hear. "Better jobs, better housing, better mental health support." I knew Black Rome would run and tell everyone what I said, bad or good. He had a lot of the kids' ears at the time. I was glad when I saw, from the corner of my eye, that he was nodding as I talked.

Safe Streets received national attention a year later, when

CNN aired a special called *Guns: A Country Divided*. I met with Carol Costello in the garden on Port Street, where the McElderry Park Community Association and the Amazing Grace Lutheran Church hold their yearly picnic. We sat in the garden and had a serious conversation about gun control.

What I had learned from Safe Streets, I told her, is that no one will put down their guns and drugs until you give them some other way to survive. Dudes who are financially secure don't need to acquire money through violence. I told her about the partnership Safe Streets had with All-State Career School, which trained people to drive trucks or repair heaters and air conditioners. I told her about the driving school program Faruq set up when he realized most of the dudes we wanted to help didn't have a license.

Faruq and I had not been able to figure out why more people weren't signing up. There were a hundred spots and it was completely free. When T.E. signed up and then told me he was going to quit a week later, I decided to go with him to the next class. I sat right next to him, and pointed at the board.

"Just copy everything that's up there," I told him.

He squinted up at the board, then looked back at me. That's when I realized he didn't know what it said.

This turned out to be the case for about half the guys in the room. Some quit the class and signed up for a G.E.D. program, but a lot of dudes just quit and went back to the streets.

My point, I told Carol Costello, was that you can't just take the guns and walk away. You have to stay, and fill the hole you've created, and sometimes that takes a lot of layers.

A couple days later, I was headed back toward the city on Route 70 when I got a call from my cousin Mansy in California. He told me he had seen me on CNN talking about guns. Later that day, my man Bok called me from prison and told me same thing. Then Shang called me, and then my sister Quanza. Everyone I knew had seen it; I got a lot of calls from federal prison that week.

33

Mediation

One evening in the early fall of 2008, Bodie asked me to bring him to the Safe Streets office on Monument. He said he wanted a word with Faruq.

Y'all should know by now that when Bodie said he wanted a word with somebody, that could go a couple different ways. I knew how he felt about Safe Streets. For the past year, every time I came around his place, he had given me the same warning—*don't bring those Safe Streets motherfuckers around, I ain't safe*. And I knew how he felt about Faruq. I hadn't forgotten the long silence between us in prison.

But when I pressed Bodie on his business with Faruq, his answer surprised me. He didn't want to threaten Faruq; he wanted to thank him. Bodie's daughter Geneen had been charged with possession of a handgun a few weeks prior. Geneen had spent the weeks following her arrest volunteering for Safe Streets, urging young women away from gun violence. When her court date rolled around, Faruq and I accompanied her to court and Faruq attested to her community service in front of the judge, so instead of getting jail time, Geneen received probation. Bodie had just learned of Faruq's role in his daughter's sentencing.

I parked in the lot behind the building and led Bodie to the glass door between Liberty Tax and Kennedy Fried Chicken on Monument Street. Searching for the keys in my pocket, I looked over at my uncle. His face was completely blank. I opened the door, and together we walked up the stairs and through the doorway of the office.

Faruq was sitting at the round conference table in the middle of the room, head bent over a newspaper. He looked up when we walked in, and I watched as the two men shook hands. It was an extraordinary moment for me—Leon Faruq and Uncle Bodie in the same room and they ain't beefing.

When doing a mediation, there are a couple ground rules. First, you have to make sure that the guys actually want to meet. Otherwise, they'll stay on the defensive. I knew Faruq didn't have a problem with Bodie. In fact, I suspect he took Geneen under his wing in order to win Bodie over, and win me over by association. I knew Bodie had a problem with Faruq, but like I said, this whole thing was his idea.

Second, you have to pick a neutral spot. I don't know if the Safe Streets office counted as neutral in this case, but I decided to step outside so that Faruq and Bodie could talk in private. I walked down Monument towards Rose Street, and then circled the block. By the time I got back to the office, the common area was empty.

"Hamza?" I called. He was working in a back room.

"What's up Tater?" he called back.

"Where'd Faruq and Bodie go?"

Hamza's face appeared in the doorframe.

"I think they said they were going to dinner."

Bodie never told me exactly what he and Faruq talked about that night. But the next time we spoke, he told me something else. He said that when we were in prison together, he saw me going through a transition, and he envied it. He saw me becoming a teacher, becoming a follower of Islam, becoming at peace. He really wanted that.

"My image, though," he said. "It would never have survived."

34

The End

It was Kisha who first pointed out to me that Faruq looked unwell. We were standing on the corner of an intersection facing the center, where Faruq stood with a bullhorn to his lips. Even though it was the dead of winter, people were gathered on all four corners; some spilled onto the street. This was a shooting response, and like most, it took place at the scene of the shooting.

"Have you seen Faruq lately?" she whispered to me. "He doesn't look good."

I looked at the man with the bullhorn. For the first time, I noticed that his winter coat looked too big for his body, even though it was the same one he'd worn for years. Above it, his face was pale and ashy. He was fifty-eight years old.

I knew Faruq was sick when we were in prison. He always complained that it was hard for him to pee, that he had some kind of prostate issue. But still I brushed Kisha off. "He's all right," I said. "You just used to being around sick people all day." Kisha had gotten her nurse's certification and was working at a nursing home.

"Yeah, exactly, Tater," she whispered back. "That's how I know."

Over the next few months, Faruq came down with one thing after another. He had pneumonia, then the flu, and then pneumonia again before the first cough even went away.

It was June and I was driving eastbound down Northern Parkway when I got the call from Sister Noni, Faruq's wife. She told me Faruq was in the hospital. I asked her which one. She said Sinai, the one I just passed. I pulled a U-turn at the next light.

What is it about hospital beds that make people look so small? Even with his body splayed on the mattress, Faruq took up hardly any room on it. His skin was darker than usual and his eyes were yellow. When I said hello, he gazed at a point just to my left.

Then he started mumbling—a loud mess of noises that sounded like he was trying to talk. Trying to tell me something. It scared me and I left the room. When I came back, he was calm. This time he stared directly at me, and I knew it wouldn't be long before he passed.

I pulled up a chair next to his bed. I told him I didn't want to see him like this.

"But I got you, man," I said. "With this Safe Streets shit. I got you. You ain't even gotta worry about it, brother, I got you."

Faruq had no response. The room was silent, and for just a moment, the world was still.

Epilogue
March, 2018

This morning, like most mornings, I glance at the building across the street as I walk into the City Health Department. The Living Classrooms Foundation stands exactly where 125 building stood twenty-two years ago. The two steadiest jobs I've ever had, less than one hundred feet apart. This morning, like most mornings, I look up from the building across the street to the sky. Like *God, you played a lot of games with me.* Down at the corner, a Ronald McDonald House sits on the Lafayette Raiders' football field.

Brother Hamza is the director of Safe Streets now. We have almost thirty violence interrupters. We have sites in Cherry Hill, Park Heights, McElderry Park, and Sandtown-Wincester, where Freddie Gray lived and died.

I helped pull together a team of interrupters for each site based on who I knew in each area. Park Heights was easy—Uncle Rebo had lived in the neighborhood for the last three decades, so I recruited all of his son's friends. Since its implementation in February 2013, the Park Heights site has gone an entire year without a homicide twice.

Between the years of 2012 and 2016, we also had a site in Mondawmin, where Uncle Bodie was one of our most successful interrupters. The Safe Streets Mondawmin site went all of 2014 without a homicide. But it was shut down after the police arrested Bodie with ten grams of heroin and one of his supervisors[7] with a gun. I had heard through the grapevine that a certain police unit was targeting Safe Streets Mondawmin, so I wasn't surprised when it happened. The Baltimore City

---

[7] Levar Mullen, who just came home, following the indictment of Daniel Hersl.

Police had, and still have, a problem with ex-offenders running a program like ours.

Walking into my office, the first thing I see is a framed diploma from Sojourner-Douglass. When I finally walked across that stage in 2013, it had been seven or eight years since I watched my dope shop from the window. And it had been over two decades since I last earned a diploma, the one my mother had to bring to me in jail. This time around, I accepted the piece of paper with my own two hands while my family watched from the crowd. My mother told me after the ceremony that she was excited for the next person to ask after her son. She wouldn't have to say, "They moved him to another jail," or "I just got a letter from him," or "He's on lock up." Now she could say, "Oh, he just graduated with his Bachelor's degree." That meant everything to me.

The following semester, I enrolled again to get my Master's in Public Administration. I had been promoted at Safe Streets and I knew I needed to learn how to finance non-profits in case Safe Streets ever folded. In June 2015, I walked across the stage a second time. As it turned out, I got my Master's just in time; Sojourner-Douglass College went bankrupt later that month. Mine was the last graduating class.

At my desk, I sit down and jiggle the computer mouse. An unread email from Melvin Russell appears at the top of my inbox. He wants to meet to talk about an upcoming documentary about gun violence in Baltimore.

I hadn't seen Officer Russell for years until a couple years ago, when he took over the police department's chaplain corps. He is actually a pastor himself, and was responsible for expanding the role of police chaplains. Chaplains used to just speak at police graduations and stuff, but now they do ride-alongs, and help police stay calm when otherwise they might get violent. The chaplains also work with trauma victims, which is where Safe Streets comes in. Sometimes they want to partner with us, and we'll do a community event together. Nothing major, though; you know we can't be seen affiliating with the police too much.

Melvin Russell loves Safe Streets. He's one of the only high-ranking officers who sees the program as an ally. When he needs to get in contact with somebody on the street, he'll call me, and I'll relay the message. Crucially, information only goes one way between police and Safe Streets. *Look,* they'll tell us, *we heard such-and-such are beefing, if y'all could go up there and squash it for us?* Never the other way around.

A few years ago, I ran into Officer Ogden, a.k.a. Chuck Norris, at the gas station on the corner of Fayette and Central. After exchanging a little small talk, I reminded him of the McDonald's heist I was blamed for as a teenager.

"You locked me up right down there," I said, pointing down the street at where the McDonald's used to be. Chuck Norris looked embarrassed.

"Ah, man, I'm sorry about that," he said, squinting slightly. "How about I buy you a beer?"

"How about you pay my mother back that thousand dollar bail?" I was only half-joking, but after a few moments of awkward silence, I decided to laugh it off. We said our goodbyes, and he drove off in his cruiser.

Not all of my relationships with Baltimore City Police have been repaired, though. I haven't forgotten the morning two years ago when I woke up to a status at the top of my Facebook feed—"damn! They up in the Safe Streets office at 5 in the morning"—and had to hustle to the office on Monument Street. There had been a raid overnight. Hersl's crew, cruising around East Baltimore in the wee hours of the morning, had allegedly spotted a gray van outside the Safe Streets building that "matched the description" of one used in a robbery earlier that night. So Hersl pulled up, broke into the office, and "found" two guns in plain view. This "find" provided probable cause for his squad to conduct a full-on raid, lasting into the afternoon, and resulting in further "discovery" of guns and drug paraphernalia in a bookbag. Nine people were arrested outside the Safe Streets East office that day, including two Safe

Streets employees.

The possession charges were eventually dismissed, mostly because Hersl's affidavit didn't make any sense. For one thing, surveillance footage placed my homeboy Dorsey's gray van at the Royal Farms on Pulaski Highway at the time of the alleged robbery. For another, the affidavit claims that whoever called in the robbery reported "his gun, his bookbag, his scale, and all his drugs" stolen. I'm willing to bet no one has ever called the Baltimore City Police to report their gun and drugs stolen. Hersl was getting sloppy—probably why he and his boys are all over *The Sun's* front pages right now.[8]

Of the twelve Hotboys locked up seventeen years ago, half are still serving time. A few came home and got killed or locked up again. Maurice became a hospital responder for Safe Streets. D.J. is coming home soon. But the one I'm most anxious to see is my man Leon. In a terrible accident a few years ago, I hit his little son with my truck and Lil Leon was killed. I don't know what our reunion will be like.

I'm starting to go to a bad place in my head when my phone buzzes in my pocket and pulls me out of my thoughts. It's my mother. She wants me to come to O'Donnell Heights projects, where she lives now.

"They set my bush on fire!" she tells me when I answer.

"Who did?"

"Who you think?"

My mom is in an ongoing battle with the little dealers who hang out in the courtyard outside her building. She's been spraying AJAX cleaner on the wall so that they won't sit there. Now they seem to have retaliated.

I try not to laugh. When they were demolishing the other side of O'Donnell Heights, my mom had instructed Pop and I to go across the street to dig up a flower bush, carry it over, and

---

[8] Daniel Hersl and the rest of the Gun Trace Task Force were finally found guilty of planting evidence, among other charges, in February 2018. Hersl now faces up to sixty years in prison.

plant it next to her porch. She wanted to stop the traffic going through her yard. Now there was a burning bush outside her window. Wasn't that supposed to be proof of God's presence?

"Are you okay?" I ask.

"I'm fine. I just want you to know how they look in case something happens..."

I tell her I'll be over after work.

I'm not worried about my mom. She has always been a gangster. She writes and receives mail from prisons all over the country. Everybody knows Miss Carlene from Lafayette projects. Shang, Woody, and Tater's mom is what they call her.

Now J.T. is at my door, reminding me we have a presentation in Dr. Webster's class at Johns Hopkins in twenty minutes. As I follow him out, I glance at the wall above my desk, where hangs the yellow piece of paper that my mother gave me when I left for prison. The paper is crinkly and soft now, but the words are still visible. It reads:

> *Go placidly amid the noise and haste,*
> *and remember what peace there may be in silence*
> *As far as possible without surrender*
> *be on good terms with all persons.*
>
> *Speak your truth quietly and clearly;*
> *and listen to others,*
> *even the dull and the ignorant;*
> *they too have their story.*

I think Pop taught us well—despite his shortcomings.

Made in the USA
Monee, IL
29 January 2021